THE POWER OF STORIES

Mythodrama: Conflict Management
and Group Psychotherapy with Children
and Adolescents Using Stories

Allan Guggenbühl

Zurich Lecture Series in Analytical Psychology

ISAPZURICH

Volume 7

CHIRON PUBLICATIONS · ASHEVILLE, NORTH CAROLINA

www.ChironPublications.com

Interior and cover design by Danijela Mijailovic
Printed primarily in the United States of America.

ISBN 978-1-68503-145-9 paperback
ISBN 978-1-68503-146-6 hardcover
ISBN 978-1-68503-147-3 electronic
ISBN 978-1-68503-148-0 limited edition paperback

Library of Congress Cataloging-in-Publication Data

Names: Guggenbühl, Allan, author.
Title: The power of stories : mythodrama: conflict management and group psychotherapy with children and adolescents using stories / Allan Guggenbühl.
Description: Asheville, North Carolina : Chiron Publications, [2023] | Series: Zurich lecture series in analytical psychology ; volume 7 | Includes bibliographical references. | Summary: "Often lips are sealed, and delicate topics avoided, when children or adolescents are in a conflict situation or have experienced a trauma. Psychologists, psychotherapist, teachers are challenged and must find alternative ways to connect to the individual or group. Talking alone is not sufficient. In this book-Volume 7 of the Zürich Lecture Series-a therapeutic method and conflict management approach is presented, which is successfully employed in group work with children and adolescents in despair or in a conflict situation. Mythodramas main focus are specially selected stories, which mirror the issues of the respective group, connect to the issues of the group, and serve as an entrance to the imaginal. The book describes how the stories are selected, told, enacted, and linked to the issues and concerns of the group or individual. Mythodrama is a potent method, based on Jungian psychology, which helps groups to move on, express their emotions, concerns, and get motivated to find solutions. Mythodrama has successfully been applied in groups consisting of traumaticised children or adolescents, violent youth, bullies, victims of aggression, adolescents with identity crises, etc. Mythodrama is also a method which is employed in conflict management in schools. The key elements of Mythodrama are Stories, Play, Imagination, Drama, and Concrete Changes"— Provided by publisher.
Identifiers: LCCN 2023030706 (print) | LCCN 2023030707 (ebook) | ISBN 9781685031459 (paperback) | ISBN 9781685031466 (hardcover) | ISBN 9781685031473 (ebook) | ISBN 9781685031480 (limited edition paperback)
Subjects: LCSH: Conflict management. | Adolescent psychotherapy. | Group psychotherapy. | Jungian psychology.
Classification: LCC HM1126 .G84 2023 (print) | LCC HM1126 (ebook) | DDC 303.6/9—dc23/eng/20230724
LC record available at https://lccn.loc.gov/2023030706
LC ebook record available at https://lccn.loc.gov/2023030707

CONTENTS

INTRODUCTION

Summary

This chapter starts with an example how children fantasise themselves into the world and give meaning to themselves and the environment. Next, the role of the inner world is described and the prospect of getting in touch with them through stories. Stories are understood as bridges to the inner world of children and adolescents and are analysed in their significance for communities, but also as a link between the inner world and the realities of life.

Simmental cows graze in the field, Lake Zurich glistens in the horizon. In the background, you can hear a lawn mower and the noise of a trolley bus at the last stop of this residential neighbourhood. I unload my shopping from the back of my car and think about what the last scribble on my shopping list means. Mascarpone? Suddenly, I hear a voice behind me: "This is a dangerous area!" I am informed. "Robbers are on the rampage, have already set fire to a house on the edge of the forest!" As I turn around, another voice updates me, "Don't worry! We will protect you!"

Behind me are not policemen or vigilantes, but three 7- to 8-year-old boys! They have armed themselves with wooden swords, water pistols and a bow with arrows. It's obvious! They have a mission to fulfill! They have to take action against robbers, they inform me! "How do you know about these robbers?" I wish to know. The answers come almost simultaneously from three mouths: "Someone has observed two men sneaking to the little house by the forest. They broke in to cover their traces. Afterwards, they set the house on fire!" A boy adds excitedly that this gang of criminals even intended to kidnap someone! When I react in disbelief, the boys point towards the forest: Indeed, I can detect is a burnt-out garden shed!

The garden shed was not set on fire by robbers, it was a barbecue accident, I find out later. Nor was the neighbourhood haunted by a gang. The robbers just existed in the minds of these boys. However, the robber story circulated. Many children in the neighbourhood shared it, were convinced that these bad men really existed. Fake news? In the eyes of these children, the burnt garden shed was the ultimate proof of the activities of sinister malicious men. From the children's point of view, it was evident: Something had to be done against these villains! The 7- to 8-year-old boys were the only ones to take the threat seriously and were prepared to defend the neighbourhood!

The episode took place a few years ago in a peaceful suburban quarter. Everything seemed as it should be in that part of the time. Cars were parked according to rules on the right-hand side of the street, in the blue zone; a facility manager was scrubbing the front yard of an apartment building, a jogger had finished his round and was picking his mail out of his mailbox, a woman was disposing a municipal blue waste bag in the block's own container. A pedestrian held a dog excrement bag that contained what her dog had produced. On the first floor of the block, a teenager could be spotted behind a window. He was sitting at his desk. In short: Everyone was behaving in a socially adequate manner, with the exception of the three boys.

If an extra-terrestrial visitor were to observe the scene, it would conclude that all but the boys had a chip implanted in their brains! They abided to a superordinate system of rules. Their behaviour mirrored common habits and rules. They conformed to rules conferring to the situation they were in. They fulfilled defined functions, adapted. The boys, in contrast, did not conform. Their behaviour would probably seem odd in the eyes of an extra-terrestrial being, not conforming with societal rules and regulations. These children were driven by a fantasy. So, are imaginations incapable of imagining.

If we could scan the heads of adults, we probably would get a different picture. Their conformity is feigned. They are also immersed in fantasies. The pedestrian with the dog waste bag perhaps imagined her Pinscher biting the jogger and causing an uproar in the neighbourhood. The jogger was perhaps reminded by the dog owner of his ex-wife who always wanted the windows closed at night. The chauffeur looked at the slickness of the end-loop and perhaps put himself in the place of a truck driver roaring across an icy lake in the Yukon. The teenager was engrossed in a computer game and imagined himself as a knight in a tournament fighting over the beautiful Guinevere. In other words, adults are also driven by fantasies, but they usually distance themselves from the spontaneous images that emerge. Functionality is expected.

This attitude characterises most people. They detach themselves from their fantasies. They perceive their spontaneous images, feelings, and sensations as a threat. Fantasies cannot be controlled, but rather have a life of their own. Our inner eye recapitulates dirty scenes, fulfills sensuous wishes, recalls painful traumas, or drafts future scenarios. However, often these spontaneous ideas are perceived as fleeting thoughts, waste products of the brain without personal relevance. It would be inappropriate to act out fantasies, it would disrupt our lives. Therefore, one prefers to keep them to oneself, does not acknowledge them, represses them and only allows appropriate fantasies that conform, do not irritate.

To understand the dynamics of this phenomenon, psychology might help: a science that searches for laws, connections, motives and influencing factors of our behaviour and self-awareness. Psychology analyses regular behaviour, studies disorders, evaluates relationships, organises investigations in social conduct and tries to identify hidden motives. Psychology is based on two paths of knowledge: external observations and reflections of inner life. Empirical psychology focuses on external observation. It is committed to reality. Observations are the basis of its conclusions. Its main aim is to collect data in order to achieve evidence-based findings. Empirical science therefore conducts investigations and operates with figures and numbers. It concentrates on measurable characteristics and interpersonal behaviour patterns. Averages are calculated and significance is sought. Conclusions should be comprehensible and replicable. The objects of their studies are being photographed, filmed, recorded, or objectified through interviews and then translated into data.

Another tool to understand human beings is *introspection*. When we concentrate on inner life, we try to understand ourselves from within ourselves. The starting points of this path of knowledge are inner realities: images, fantasies, thoughts that we perceive only with our inner eye and ear. This private world cannot be objectified because it is only accessible to the inner eye and ear of the person concerned. Outsiders can neither photograph our inner life nor make a tape recording or film it. It remains hidden from the outside world. What goes on inside us can neither be seen by second persons nor recorded empirically. We are the *only* witnesses of our personal dreams, fantasies, visions, thoughts, and only we are confronted with our own emotions. Even the latest neurological techniques fail to decode a person's thoughts and fantasies. Just like the patterns of brain activity, people's inner lives each have an individual profile.

Many things that drive us, however, can only be reasonably explained by referring to the inner world. Personal reflection is important to understand our motives, attitudes, and goals. However, since our inner life cannot be transferred into data or underpinned with direct observations, we can only identify consistencies: develop theories and models that sound plausible and help us understand ourselves. They are based on memories, associations, ideas, fantasies, and feelings, which we pursue with the help of our consciousness. Often, however, the contents of our inner life have no or only a loose connection with external factors. Fantasies, as I will explain in more detail later, lead a life of their own. They can hardly be influenced. They are created by unconscious forces. We are exposed to them. A fantasy haunts us, a feeling bothers us, an idea vexes us, or an image disturbs us. The inner world has its own directors and abides to its own script. What goes on inside us often seem like anarchy, disregarding social conventions and moral concerns. Our inner world is not a reflection of external stances, but generates itself from innate dispositions, memories, and past experiences.

However, we can connect to the inner world indirectly. We have a great tool for this: *language*. Languages enable us to achieve information beyond our sensory and perceptual horizons and our personal experiences. They offer us metaphors, which help us to penetrate unknown realms. Languages help us to overcome mental limitations. We can grasp the events of our inner world as well as those of our fellow human beings linguistically. If someone describes to us that in a dream, he entered a huge concert hall dressed in white and helplessly pressed an old mobile phone until the conductor, dressed in tails and nappies, greeted him, we develop a version of this absurd scene in our head. Of course, this remains a personal version and only approximates the dreamer's ideas. However, we get an idea of what is going on inside him.

Our inner life cannot be reduced to static images like in a gallery but should be perceived as dynamic and full of surprises. It resembles a theatre. Dramas, tragedies, farces, comedies, catastrophes, romances are staged. A variety of figures appears in various scenarios. We see ourselves transported to an alp in the Bernese Oberland and dancing a tango, we are on a train to Sidney, chased by a crocodile, or we are sitting in the Pig & Whistle in Kyoto, drinking a beer while a Samurai enters, surrounded by dancing mice. Our inner life is often incomprehensible to us, sometimes fascinating and maybe irritating. At the same time, our inner life reflects the world we live in. People and scenes appear that are familiar to us, but many things remain mysterious. Why do I imagine myself blowing up Bellevue Square? What does this erotic fantasy about a work colleague mean? Deciphering our own inner life and searching for a meaning remain personal tasks for all of us. But how to capture our individual images, impressions, thoughts, insights, sensations, and feelings? How can we deal with our inner fantasies, residues, and engrams? And how can we connect this inner cacophony with the tsunami of impressions from the outside world?

The answer: with the help of stories. Humans developed the ability to capture paradoxes, irritations, fascinations, and traumas through stories.[1] Thanks to stories, personal events and inner images are connected and developed into a meaningful whole. Stories are stepping-stones or facilitators. They are created from memories, one's own knowledge, social guidelines, and are an answer to a problem or a challenge. Stories are how we try to understand ourselves, connect with others and develop communities.[2] We derive them from social myths, relational experiences, traumas, archetypal precepts, enrich them with personal experiences and calibrate them with our own attitudes. Stories use personal impressions, facts, and amplify them from one's own fantasies and expectations. They are the link between the outside and the inside world, the result of a compromise between psychological needs and the demands of adaptation of the outside world. Personal needs are placed, experienced traumas are relativised or emphasised. Stories give us an orientation.

Many stories that we develop and that fascinate us are about conflicts. They are about situations that overwhelm, stress, or irritate us. Impressions, residues of the day, experiences, and memories are processed. They are the soul's attempt to deal with difficult events or problems. Inner resources are consulted to develop a perspective. Thoughts, observations, memories, dreams, and perceptions are brought into a sequence by the story so that we can understand something and perhaps even derive meaning from an event. We then believe we understand why something happened and what it means.

Stories mobilize an important element of our existence: our imagination. It allows us to immerse ourselves in fictional worlds. Fiction frees us from the confinement of reality. We can oppose the here and now when it threatens to absorb us. This already happens with trivial events. We criticize the partner because she is late. It's just a matter of coordinating one's own movement so that one is present at a certain place at the same time, an organizational issue. "Everyone in your family is not punctual, even your father . . .", we might reproach our partner and get the answer that we ourselves come from a "fussy bourgeois family" that only has duty and order in mind. We react with family stories.

Of course, we believe them to be accurate, but often they are "truthy stories": personal stories that we claim to be true, even though they are wholly or partly fictional.[3] Even if we strive for truth and seem to quote facts, they remain fantasies. We try to distance ourselves from reality with the help of a story by transferring the corresponding challenge into another topos.

Introduction

Communities survive on stories. They make coexistence possible and strengthen solidarity among members. Companies thrive on stories to give employees a vision or a profile. Every individual also develops a personal life story from which he or she derives personal characteristics, strengths, weaknesses and exonerates dark personality traits. A personal life story is part of the self-image. It serves as orientation and often is the basis for decisions.

Stories strengthen solidarity and make living together possible. Families need stories to compensate for internal and personality differences. Stories in families often create a sense of a togetherness and grant the family members a common origin.

Now back to the opening story. The three boys felt summoned to keep the order in their neighborhood. But did they really believe in the robber story? Hardly. It is more likely that the story was a *quasi-reality* for them. It was a reality construction, as we often observe with children. The boys did not really believe that the robbers existed, but they put themselves in a state of mind that transforms the robbers into actual figures. They lived the robbers' story both emotionally and mentally. Thanks to this identification, they were able to imagine themselves mentally in the robbers' scene and understand the corresponding suspense, angst, and search for answers. They confronted themselves with an existential issue: how to deal with evil.

In this example, one purpose of the stories can be seen. They can be understood as a template of our environment but also as a container for our inner energy. They serve as a link between reality and the inner world. Thanks to their fictional character, we can indulge more in the immediacy of the moment and fathom out our existence both emotionally and mentally. Stories are a bridge between the inner world and the world outside; they empower us and enable us to act. A prerequisite, however, is an understanding of quasi-realities. While younger children regard them as a resource and rely on stories in a playful way, adults tend to reduce their meaning. It then is not about a playful representation of sequences of events and their effects, but either about fake news, facts, true stories, actualities, gossip, or inventions. When we categorize stories, there is a danger that we fail to see their function and value. Stories are a valuable addition to our lives, helping us connect inside and outside. [4] They are an invitation to engage with ourselves and the world around us. But when stories are being reified, analysed, scrutinised for their truthfulness, or judged by their literary quality, we risk distancing ourselves from them. We detach ourselves. The resonance that a story might have in us is not perceived or considered unimportant. It is not recognized that a story is also an expression of an inner event or hints at a hidden motive.

This might be the case with the individuals in the suburban neighborhood. They hesitate to develop an open story based on their challenges: The dog owner may be struggling with aggression, perhaps identifying too much with her Pinscher; the jogger has not overcome the separation from his wife; the bus driver wants to give his life a change and live out his love of adventure; and the teenager would like to have a girlfriend he can impress. They could develop and act out stories, loaded with components of their existence. Maybe this would enable them to connect to themselves and understand what is going in their lives. However, this inner resource is not accessed. Unlike many children who perceive their fantasies as a quasi-reality, adults tend to ignore them. One reason is: We must perform and meet the expectations of private and professional roles. The focus is on conforming to codes and norms. One must prove oneself, assert oneself, communicate with one's fellow human beings, maintain one's position, be empathetic and, if possible, not ruin one's own reputation. The dialogue with one's own inner self recedes into the background. This alienation seems to increase due to the digitalization of our lives. We satisfy our need for stories through films, Netflix, and media gossip. We allow ourselves to be excited, frightened, irritated, and steered by construed and often commercialized stories without engaging or questioning ourselves. We don't link our reaction to ourselves, our personal psychology. That a story might trigger a personal process is not acknowledged and has no consequences in our everyday lives. When we are mesmerized by a Netflix series or devour a novel, we don't make any personal connection. Stories are dealt with in an impersonal manner so that they don't threaten us. This way we preserve the illusion that they have nothing to do with ourselves but are pure entertainment and fulfill our need for information. The problem is: We are in danger of overlooking ourselves, our soul.

This book shows a way to creatively overcome the distance between the inner world and the outer world. The inner world is understood as a resource by which we can add depth to our own lives, recognize dangers, and gain meaning in life. The path to life requires the exploration of oneself. To approach the mystery of being, however, appropriate models and concepts are essential. Mythodrama helps children and young people to connect and come to terms with their inner world. What is going on inside them is opened with the help of stories. Stories contain symbols and images that encourage children and young people to fantasise and become aware of their emotions. Through Mythodrama, they embark on a journey to themselves with the aim of using their own potential so that they can better cope with challenges and problems. The imaginal empowers them to tackle the challenges they are confronted with in reality. The boys' robber story is an example of how this can happen. Their story enabled them to experience themselves as a group, mobilize energies, and agree on a mutual goal. Mythodrama is based on a respect for the inner world. Dealing with the inner world is a prerequisite for children and young people to cope with school and personal challenges. When the inner world is mirrored in a story, this helps children and young people, but also adults, to sort themselves out. If a narrative fits, then repressed emotions, hidden frustrations, and hopes might become conscious. For the boys, it was the robber story, which unleashed emotions. The robber narrative expressed their fantasies and aspirations. In order to comprehend the meaning, however, quasi-reality was necessary. The boys had to enact the story in their lives. In therapy, this can be done by continuing the story, by acting it out, expressing it pictorially, depicting it in a sand play, or dramatizing it. Enactments and concretizations help to derive personal meanings. A contact between inside and outside enables us to reacquaint ourselves with our own existence. The boys transferred the robber story into their everyday life, continued it and dedicated themselves to it. This quasi-reality enabled them to get to know themselves more deeply and to gain a new perspective. Whether their conclusions correspond to the actual meanings of the story is not relevant. What is crucial is that the story helped them to decipher themselves and activate mental energies.

ENDNOTES

[1] S. Pinker, *How the Mind Works*.

[2] D.S. Wilson, *Darwin's Cathedral*.

[3] J. Gottschall, *The Storytelling Animal. How Stories make us human*. p. 161ff.

[4] M. Solms, *The Hidden Spring. A Journey to the Source of Consciousness*.

1

Allowing Semi-chaos:
The Core of Group Therapy

Summary

This chapter begins with questions and challenges therapists are confronted with when trying to help and work with children or adolescents. It then introduces the basics of group psychotherapy with children and adolescents. Especially when trying to solve conflicts, we often reach our limits when relying on dialogue. Other methods are required if we want to help children and adolescents to cope with their challenges and problems and reach them. We need to connect with their inner selves and help them to discover their own resources. The second part of this chapter depicts the qualities and possibilities of the group setting. The group situation and especially the awareness of being among themselves changes the behavior of many children and young people: They open up. The chapter points out which group-dynamic aspects and which dangers must be considered, then the archetypal background of group psychotherapy is explained, which is a prerequisite for Mythodrama.

Therapy with children and adolescents.

During the initial interview with a boy whose parents have rescheduled with me at the request of the school board he says to me: "I don't know why I'm here," the eleven-year-old boy informs me out front. He looks around nervously, as if to find a way out. He is obviously uncomfortable and embarrassed. Finally, his gaze falls on a picture hanging on the wall behind me. I ask him how is getting on in school. He seems absentminded. "Very good!" he replies and brags: "I'm the brightest and most popular pupil in the whole school!" And after a pause, he adds in a more sincere tone: "Where is the island in the picture?" "In Scotland," I explain. Now the boy becomes talkative: "There are monsters in underground canals there!" he informs me and adds: "I know where they are hiding!" From that moment on a dialogue is possible.

Later, I talk to the parents. They are desperate. They love their son, but his behavior at home and at school is unbearable. In a fit of anger, he disposed of his younger sister's toys in the river near where they live. At meals, he categorically refuses to eat what is served, and in the morning, the parents often cannot persuade him to get out of bed. He refuses to go to school. According to the teachers, he is an intelligent and alert boy, but he is not controllable. He ignores instructions, is loud during lessons and makes insulting remarks. The school management is considering expelling him after some parents complained about him. The boy's parents are at a loss. The boy himself, however, is convinced that everything is fine. What bothers him, however, are his nervous parents and — according to him — the incompetent teachers.

As a child and youth psychologist, however, one often has to deal with children or adolescents whose own assessment of their problems is *diametrically* opposed to that of their environment. They do not want to acknowledge that they have problems. While parents and teachers are concerned or even distressed about their behavior or emotional state, these children or adolescents experience themselves and their situation as unproblematic. They suffer, but from their point of view, due to the circumstances. As a result, they do not see why they need to consult a psychologist.

Of course, some children and adolescents wish to talk to an outside person about their worries and problems. They appreciate the exchange with a professional helper. Often, they do not present their problem or worry but wait for the psychologist to make the first move. The reason is: Therapies for children or adolescents are often prescribed interventions. Parents, schools, or experts have advised them, or decreed them, to consult a psychologist.

In contrast to adults, children and adolescents have a vague idea of how a psychotherapist or psychologist might work, even though it was explained to them beforehand. They are involved in something unknown to them. That is why we need to relate to them what therapy is. It is not sufficient to explain to them that we are trying to help them and it's for their own good. More steps are necessary to gain their confidence. Often, they start with prejudices. In individual therapy as well as in group therapy, it is therefore essential to make the child or young person aware that we are working with them regardless of the question of guilt. Therapy is not education or a punishment for bad behavior but about finding out what is going on inside them and how they can help themselves. We try to empower children and adolescents so they can cope with their issues. Often, I ask the child or adolescent during the first session why he or she thinks they are sent to me. Many children or young people answer that their parents or school sent them to me. The adults want them to change. Some mention personal difficulties, others feel they are being victimized, and many, if not the majority, fail to recognize their part. According to them, they are blameless. These children and adolescents are not used to problematizing themselves. However, practically all children and, to a slightly lesser extent, the adolescents are open to new contacts. They are emotionally responsive and curious. Since they usually have no idea what the official reasons for their signing up with me are, I describe my state of knowledge of the problem and the expectations, which led to contacting me. If the child or young person reacts nervously or in a distressed manner, then I switch to a topic that emerges spontaneously or might interest him or her. When contacting a child or adolescent the first time, exchanging sounds is of prime importance, but the content is not that relevant. We must help the child or adolescent to arrive emotionally and connect to us.

In individual therapy, a gradual approach is recommended. I usually adapt my words and reactions to the sensitivities I perceive. I try to imagine what his or her concerns and interests are and try to formulate my words accordingly. Any topic is possible. Often, we engage in a random subject. A 12-year-old boy brought up the punitive system of his school as a topic, a girl complained about her disloyal friends, and another boy ranted about his mother. As a therapist, I concentrate on listening. If I want to establish a relationship to him or her, then I must find out how one can reach him or her. What approach is appropriate? When you work with children, it is advisable to introduce a medium in addition to words. We should give them a chance to express themselves indirectly. It can be sand play, a puppet theatre, painting, free play, or stories. Which method to choose depends not only on professional skills but also on the personality and interests of the child or adolescent. Not all children like to play or want to paint.

Individual therapy helps a child or young person to strengthen his or her self-confidence, to come to terms with traumatic experiences, and to organize internally to cope better with personal challenges. As a rule, the child or young person gradually internalizes the therapist. He or she becomes an inner figure and valuable resource with which to relate. This gives the respective child or adolescent strength to handle his or her difficulties better, be it depression, fears, behaviour problems, or frustrations.

However, many problems in childhood or adolescence are results of the external circumstances. They must prove themselves at school, compete with colleagues, meet expectations of the school or family. They must prove themselves as social beings, learn to function in a community, assert and distinguish themselves. Often, their roles in school and at home don't match. They move on different stages, which adhere to distinct codes and rules. In both scenes, they must adapt. Due to this process, their own sensitivities, complexes, or problems are intermixed with difficulties in adapting. Adaption demands a lot of energy and is a necessity during childhood. The danger among children or young people is that they externalize their difficulties. Instead of looking at themselves, fears are acted out, insecurities are seen because of unempathetic grown-ups, and aggressions are seen as legitimate defenses or despair as a result of an unfulfilled wish. Instead of looking at themselves and starting to look for causes and connections, the issue is attributed to other people or situations. The teacher is "to blame," the colleagues are "mean," or the parents are not understanding. As a result, these children or adolescents are confronted with demands they do not comprehend. The school, colleagues, and often parents demand that they behave! They experience their problems, and as a result, they must deal with a collective that wants something from them. They experience themselves as part of a group or community that sets its own rules and codes and is characterised by a special dynamic. They experience the power, the attraction, and the dangers of the collective. They get to know themselves as members of a community, suffer because of mutual difficulties, and are often under stress because they must adapt. They also must develop competences to deal with this situation and become resilient.

Basics of group therapy

This is where the significance of group psychotherapy comes in. Individual therapy and group therapy have a lot in common. Both should not be guided by the norms and rules set up by the school as representative of the collective but should value the child or adolescent as an *independent* subject, with his or her own views, thoughts, emotions, and interests. Even more important: In individual and in group therapy, the inner life of the child or young person is of prime importance. The therapist looks for means to bring them into line with the demands of society or the collective. In contrast to individual therapies, group therapies offer *arenas* in which children or young people can explore not only their own challenges but also how to deal with their collective. This process is made possible because of the specific qualities of the group setting.

Our emotions, behaviour, perception, and thoughts are influenced by the social context in which we live. Our immediate environment affects us more then we might believe. What is revealed about oneself depends therefore on the respective counterparts. Children express needs to their parents that they do not admit to schoolmates and present themselves differently to teachers than they do to siblings. If the relationship is characterized by trust and a certain intimacy, then children and adolescents are more likely to admit their vulnerable sides. Conversely, in contact with nonfamily persons, characteristics manifest themselves that hardly ever appear in the family context or individual therapy. Depending on what masks are required in the particular social context, needs are masked, disclosed, or denied. At school, one does not admit that one is not well but annoys the teacher or refuses to cooperate. The behaviour and experiences of children and young people reflect their social environment.

In group settings, children and adolescents experience themselves differently than they do in school or in individual settings. Groups often trigger fantasies that children or adolescents hide in individual settings or at school. The language changes, too. Especially older children tend to adapt to the jargon of their peers. The group setting also reduces the dependencies on the adults. When they know they are among themselves, children and young people restrain themselves less. Because they don't feel they are being observed, they are more likely to follow the group groove. For all these reasons, the behaviour of many children and young people in a group setting therefore differs from the impression they make at school but often also in an individual setting or at home. What happens evolves from the encounter with colleagues. Motives that they otherwise conceal emerge. They experience themselves differently because they perceive themselves as members of a collective. Their own temperament becomes apparent to them, and, in the case of young people, their personal identity develops. Since they encounter a wide variety of personalities in the group, they are also confronted with their limits. Therefore, reflection and processing of spontaneous behaviour and group dynamics are crucial. The following pages describe some specific challenges of group work.

The qualities of semichaotic sessions in group psychotherapy

"Dead boring!" a girl says snappishly to a boy as he brags about his successes in Fortnite. Meanwhile, two boys have built a castle with pillows and two chairs and hidden in it. They want to be found. One girl is offended because her colleague claims she has no friends at school. Meanwhile, a shout is heard from the second group room, the disco room: A boy has seized a stick and is miming a karate fighter, while another boy is tugging at the group leader's shirt. He is desperate to tell him something.

Group therapy sessions are not always calm and well-organized. They can get loud and chaotic. Leading a group therefore means to be prepared for surprises. As a group leader, you must run around, mediate, intervene, coax, calm, command, explain, tell a joke, mark boundaries, and above all, have an extra eye in the back of your head. When you finally rest, exhausted after a turbulent session, you might ask yourself: Why do you endure all this?

The children or young people, as well as the group leader, are confronted with collective dynamics. These can only be understood when they perceive the group as a distinct psychological entity. Groups develop their own profiles and offer specific challenges. In contrast to school, these groups are not disciplined by rules or subjected to a pedagogy. Therapists therefore experience situations that can challenge, anger, and unnerve them. Often one loses the overview and has the feeling of losing control. A child freaks out because she has lost in a game, a girl wantonly tears a notebook from a colleague, or a teenager stubs out a cigarette on a colleague's neck at the beginning of a group. One witnesses behaviour that neither the children nor young people concerned, nor the parents nor the school, mentioned.

In contrast to the individual setting, several pairs of eyes are directed at the children or young people. This situation influences the behaviour and mood of the children or young people. They imagine themselves on a stage and often present themselves differently than at school, at home or in the individual setting. They struggle to define their own role within the group. For the group leader, it is therefore revealing how the members of the group introduce and position themselves. How do they present themselves? How do they want to be seen? What stories do they relate, and what position do they aspire to? Behaviour can be tried out within the group. Many children make a shy impression at first but subsequently let off steam in the following sessions; others seem dismissive at first but with time behave cooperatively and sociably; and still others tell stories and brag.

Language: Discourse in the group

The children and young people reveal a lot about themselves in the group as time passes. They share their experiences, their problems, and traumas. "My teacher hates me!" complains a girl, or a boy says that he is always settling disputes among colleagues. For the group leader, it is often not easy to distinguish between actual problems, experiences, boasts, or fabrications. Often the group dynamics determine the possible range of topics. Certain problems or accusations come to the fore. Everyone complains about their parents' behaviour or insinuates problematic motives against the teachers. For example, in one session, a participant in the girls' group described in a low voice that her teacher ignored her when she raised her hand. She also claimed that he had deliberately excluded her from a school trip! She maliciously added that it was highly suspicious how he behaved. He had written her personal text messages afterwards, signed "dearest regards!" The other participants in the girls' group are horrified and report similar experiences with teachers. It is unclear, though, whether these are insinuations. In a group for the improvement of social skills, a boy complained that he had to "do all the housework," had no free time at all, and was repeatedly confined to the basement as punishment.

In cases like that, the group leader understandably feels compelled to act. In the first case, the group leader contacted the school, and in the second case, she raised the issue of punishment in talks with the parents. In the case of the unjust teacher, it turned out that he had excluded the girl from the school trip because she had repeatedly helped herself to the class funds. The money had been collected for excursions. He wrote her a text message after another incident. During an independent group work, she disappeared, and nobody knew where she was. In the case of the boy, the parents were able to convincingly present that he did not have to run the household and they did not lock him in the cellars.

Before acting, it is important to remember that language is not only used for communication but also for positioning oneself. With their own statements, children and young people strive for a position in the group, seek attention or want to distract attention from themselves. Not all statements made by children or young people should be taken at face value. Preliminary information helps the group leader in such a situation. He or she takes the children's or young people's descriptions seriously but compares them with the information he or she gets before the group starts or after having contacted the school or parents.

Qualifying the participants' self-representation

Children and young people are prone to self-deception.[1] When they know themselves to be the centre of attention, they often speak with a different tongue. They protect themselves by hiding problematic behaviors or the opposite, by showing off. When they suppress their problematic behavior, they search for causes in their environment, and they might blame other people or the circumstances. In many groups, unwritten rules start to establish themselves in the group. It becomes de rigueur rule to emphasize one's own innocence and to present oneself as a victim or a hero. For the same reason, many children or adolescents also erase experiences that embarrass them from their memory during group sessions. The image of themselves they present then does not reflect their personality but the way one must depict oneself in the group.

The events that children or young people report may not be true, but they contain clues about the issues and concerns that participants associate with the group. They reveal the basic psychological attitude that dominates in the group. Is the victim role popular? Does one want to appear as a rebel or to be nosy. The dynamics of a group can also mean that only certain topics accepted by the whole group are talked about.

Multiple contacts as a resource

Group psychotherapy offers participants various contacts. The child or adolescent is not only confronted with one counterpart but can choose between different personalities. It is interesting to see with whom a child bonds, which contacts he or she avoids, and with whom tensions arise. The way a child or young person reacts to the other members shows his or her ability to deal with diversity. In larger groups, members are sure to meet characters that do not suit them. How does he or she react? Does he or she behave pragmatically? Does she or he express rejection directly or hold the respective emotion back? The social skills of the child or adolescent become apparent in the way he or she establishes contact. In my experience, the observations of the group leaders usually correspond to the descriptions of the teachers. Whom a child or young person makes contact with or argues with might give the group leader a hint, what motives influence their behavior. The multiple contacts are therefore a valuable resource for the group work: For the group leader, it is informative how relationships develop, how coalitions form, and where tensions arise.

Transferences

The transferences that children or young people develop are also interesting. Often, they refer to relationships from the past. Suppressed affects, feelings, expectations, and desires are transferred to new social relationships and therefore reactivated. They express themselves in the fantasies that the children or young people develop about themselves and their group mates. The roles they assign to each other in the imaginary journeys and in the play contain clues to possible projections or the externalization of unconscious themes. The children or adolescents fill the contacts with other group members or the group leaders with meanings from their personal history. A boy looks for a father figure in a group leader, a girl elevates a group member to a "best friend," or a group member is spontaneously rejected by a child. However, projections are not only triggered by the in-group contacts but also by the group itself. Groups develop an idea of who they are. The group becomes a projection medium. The group participants ascribe characteristics and a history to their group, whereby the ideas can be very different. Some children see the group as a substitute for their family. The group leader represents the parents. The children then seek closeness, regress, and vie for the attention of the group leader. However, transferences can lead to certain events or topics being systematically hidden or emphasized.

The profile that the group gives itself reflects psychological needs. The children and young people project into the group characteristics and events that they miss or repress in their lives. Often the children or young people feel like a conspiratorial clique. They experience themselves as rebels who share secrets and are cheeky. The separation from the adults is staged. A group of "bad boys," for example, gave themselves hero status and glorified their deeds.

When we work with children or adolescents, we are faced with disputes, incompatibilities, and dissonances. Especially when working with children, we are confronted with inexplicable outbursts of anger, heated discussions about nothing, or suddenly being blamed without knowing why. Young people might be convinced that they are not being understood and are unaffected by counterarguments. Such conflicts are an important element of group work. Challenges should not be confused with hard-core conflicts. Common to both challenges and conflicts is that we get tense, agitated, and often anxious. We adopt a fighting stance.

In group work, we encounter countless challenging situations: Children avoid us suddenly, are cheeky, cheat, or refuse to cooperate. As a group leader, you often make an extra effort and concentrate on the problem. We rely on professional guidelines and routines. We might try to calm down an aggressive child with soothing words, break up a game that is threatening to get out of hand, or separate two group participants, which don't get along with each other.

Conflicts are more intense. The problem: We get personally involved. Because we are challenged on a personal level, there is a danger that we reach our limits. While we maintain our professional attitude in challenging situations, we might lose our pretense. Nerves are on edge; we curse the child or young person in question and are disappointed. We are not only offended but also feel aggressive impulses emerging, feel desperate, helpless, and realize that our perception is narrowing. We detect and ponder the conflict. Often, we get distressed. When a youngster spits in your face, a child deliberately tears up your new jacket, or steals money from your wallet it is not easy to remain calm. The conflict mode is triggered. We are annoyed. Moments like that can be a turning point, though. Conflicts reveal personality traits that we otherwise hide or fail to detect with someone else.

Weaknesses and complexes become apparent to oneself and to one's environment, which is not always a bad thing. The relationship might deepen. For example, in aftermath of the conflict, you realize that you really care about the fate of a child or young person. You connect with the child or young person on a more emotional level.

However, in conflict situations, group leaders often conclude that the group member in question has gone too far, been too aggressive, or mean to other members, and you consider whether he or she should be *excluded* from the group. This may be necessary in rare cases, but group exclusion should remain the last resort. Often a behavior or character trait manifests itself in the conflict that was previously hidden but is important for the therapeutic work.

Conflicts tear us apart, but they can also bring us closer to a fellow being. We get to know his or her complexes. In misbehavior, traits are expressed that we previously have not acknowledged or valued. The masks were dropped. Group psychotherapy is an opportunity to integrate problematic personality aspects. For example, maybe it is possible to redirect the energy that appeared in an aggressive outburst and used in a more civilised way. Or: Verbal injuria reveal the ability of the respective person to connect to a collective by using strong words. But maybe we can help him or her to do it in a more civilised way. It is the duty of the group leader to help the child or young person find alternatives.

Addressing and reflecting on personal weaknesses or problematic behaviour in the group setting is important. However, this might be embarrassing for the child concerned. We all have difficulty admitting personal weaknesses or problematic features spontaneously because the first thing we rescue in a conflict is our own immaculate self-image. This happens to the children and young people as well as to the group leaders. The latter often do not want to take any risks. They fear they might jeopardize the relationship of trust that they have built up with the child or young person and therefore avoid addressing the problem outright. Since children and adolescents are almost always convinced that they "can't help it," it is difficult for group leaders to debate such personal topics with the respective child or adolescent. The group leader must switch to indirect strategies. Indirect means to invite children or adolescents to draw, paint, do a drama, or engage in sand play.

Because it is difficult to address sensitive issues out front, Mytho-drama employs stories, play, and imagination, as I explain later in this book. Mythodrama is a way of addressing problematic behaviour or traits without challenging the child's or young person's self-image or shaming them. You address the problematic behaviour without hurting the child.

Shadow contents

Conflicts confront us with our shadow. We get acquainted with personality parts, complexes that we tend to exclude in our self-image but which nevertheless pursue us. We are dealing with unconscious components of our personality that influence behaviour, perception, and emotions. These shadow motives might derive from traumata we fail to acknowledge, repressed hopes, bottled-up anger, or ambitions. The point is, though, they affect us unconsciously and influence our thoughts and actions. We are not aware of these hidden motives because they do not concur with our worldview, are embarrassing to us, and contradict our values. We are ashamed of them or have not even recognized them. For example, we might be convinced that we are a good listener and always helpful when someone is in need. We then search automatically for evidence in the past that confirms that trait. We evaluate our personal lives. We then remember a conversation with a colleague during which we listened attentively. Our memory relates no other story.

However, our memory might deceive us. If we could turn back the time, we might draw completely different conclusions. We might have even dominated the conversation, talking about ourselves and not allowing any pause. We believe we were good listeners because our colleague had to interrupt us several times and force us to listen a bit. We interpret our behaviour and experiences according to what we expect of ourselves. The result: The shadow content remains hidden from us. This is usually not a problem because the environment participates in our deceptive maneuvers. The colleague probably does not dare give us any feedback or does not really care. We can continue to adhere to our convictions.

The shadow content is often a negative trait, something we are not proud of. We have difficulty admitting that we are a control freak, stingy, egomaniacal, power-hungry, or narcissistic. In conflicts, however, self-deception often no longer works. A shadow issue emerges violently and becomes a problem for oneself and the environment. Other people might react angrily. Why does he grope? Why does she betray her colleagues? Why is he so full of himself? The ugly personality traits become an issue. However, shadow issues can also be positive. We may behave more empathetically, socially, adaptively, and with more originality than we are aware of. These features or qualities appear in some persons during conflicts. When they are in a prudent mode, they repress their shadow quality because of low self-esteem, fear, or lack of personal strategies. In conflicts, these defenses collapse.

Working through conflicts and shadow issues is a core element of group work. Instead of excluding the children or young people or deciding on reprimands, we should try to identify the background of conflicts. It is important to recognise possible causes, repressed contents, and help the person concerned to find a way to find an arrangement with himself or herself. Conflicts are an opportunity to investigate the depths of one's own soul and to make a new start. Sleepless nights cannot be avoided, though.

However, it does not always need a tangible conflict. Often irritations are sufficient: small incidents that catch your eye or annoy you. They are perhaps a hint to repressed shadow contents. Most of the time what we are angry about has to do with ourselves. A young person in the girls group was regularly upset about a colleague who spoke badly about others. At almost every group meeting she would pick on this "bitch." Only with time did she and we realize that she was that bitch. She had to lash out at colleagues so that she was able to distance herself emotionally from them and not have to deal with her corresponding shadow content. She projected her shadow onto her environment.

For group psychotherapy to be successful, the shadow must be considered. However, shadow motives are usually not the only reason for conspicuous behaviour or decisions. When we say or do something, it is often due to various motives. If we block out our shadow parts, however, the subjective assessment of ourselves threatens to become one-sided. Every therapist needs a little Schopenhauerian misanthropy to be effective.

The outside world is watching

In Mythodrama sessions, the leader makes external references. He or she introduces to a child or young person what he or she has obtained as information from teachers, parents, the police, or the child and adult protection authority (CESP). External information from third parties is thus deliberately shared, in contrast to most individual therapies. One reason for this approach is to make the children and adolescents aware that the therapist is not only committed to them, but also to people in their environment. The outside world is involved. The other group members also hear what the parents or school authorities believe is the problem. However, it is important to note that these external views are not simply adopted by the therapist but are also questioned.

The dissociation of one's own shadow is the reason why the social environment of the patients or group participants is considered in mythodrama. The incidents and problems of the participants are recapitulated because they often express personality parts that are not included in their self-image. Bringing in information from the outside is a first step in coming to terms with the shadow content. In this way, the group leaders signal that the reference to reality is important to them. However, it is not a matter of searching for the truth and a criminalistic processing of what happened. Rather, external reports are considered mental movers—valuable inputs that lead to deep thinking. Often, they contain elements that contradict the participants' self-descriptions. Often, they are denied by the child or young person concerned: "It's not true at all that I gave him the finger!" The vehemence of the answer can be an indication that the child's relationship to the person to whom the obscene gesture was addressed is charged with issues, which are hidden out of shame or in order to preserve the self-image. Reproaches, analyses, clarifications, colportage, insinuations, and accusations by caregivers and outside authorities can therefore be understood as attempts to approach the shadow content of the person concerned.

Basis of mythodramatic group therapy

After a while, the members of a group experience themselves as a community. Because they share worries, hopes, and problems, a sense of unity develops. Common issues bond the group members together. They might realise that they are not alone in suffering because of an alcoholic father, the divorce of their parents, or involvement in a violent scene. At the group meetings, they can divulge their experiences and discuss coping strategies. They share grief and contemplate remedies not only with the group leader but also with fellow participants.

Mythodrama, as I describe it in this book, aims to help children or young people cope with their problems with the environment or with themselves. It depends on the leadership whether the group experience is of any help to them. The group leaders must not only concentrate on the topics of the group but also need to address the concerns of the individual child or young person. Most likely, she or he identifies events in the environment or past that have left traces in the psyche of the boy or girl. The group leader identifies incidents or situations that had a pathologizing influence on the development of the child or young person. The boy still suffers because of the nasty divorce of his parents or from a trauma as a refugee fleeing to Switzerland.

We all tend to concentrate on events and situations that are striking, strange, bizarre, extraordinary, or amoral. The danger is that we over-estimate the influence of these events, which might have happened or been retrogradely construed. We seek sensations. We identify problematic situations and relationships based on guiding ideas of what life or an environment should ideally look like. We orient ourselves to notions of normality.[2] If we find something that deviates from our conception, we regard it as a possible cause for a conflictual situation. The young person would not be violent if his father had not left the family or if the farm where the family lived had not burnt down.

This approach implies that the dysfunction or problem might be inexistent if the circumstances at the time had been different or a certain event had not in fact happened. If the child had not been abused or had been loved more, then he or she would be confident and less aggressive today. We orientate ourselves on references that are not verifiable but nevertheless sound plausible. We make connections based on our professional knowledge but also on current diagnoses of the zeitgeist. Our reflections reflect collectively accepted patterns of explanation. What is discussed among colleagues, in our profession, in professional journals, at congresses, and in talk shows is used as an explanatory template.

However, because of the multiple contexts described above, objectivity in a strictly empirical sense is not possible in psychotherapy. There are too many factors and correlations that cannot be empirically verified. Moreover, psychotherapy always operates with zeitgeist themes and allows itself to be influenced by trends. After the novel *Sybil*[3] on multiple personality disorders was published and became a sensational success, hundreds of therapists detected this disorder in their patients, just as Alice Miller's[4] analysis of the drama of the gifted child caused a furor and was subsequently cited as an explanatory template in countless therapies. Today actually, it may be diagnoses such as autism spectrum diagnosis, borderline, ADHD, burnout, or early childhood sexual abuse.[5] However, the hallmark of these diagnoses is that they convince and help thousands of patients, whether child or adult. As a result of the diagnosis, they are prepared to work on themselves.

Archetypal group psychotherapy

In Mythodrama, however, it is assumed that we are not the exclusive product of our biography and social environment but also of endogenous motives. They are understood as congenital dispositions that strive for realisation. Specific attitudes, possible interests, and strategies are laid in our laps and then shaped by culture. Our personal profile is designed by demands, talents, weaknesses, and a temperament that we cannot attribute to conditioning and enculturation. As a result, we are drawn to subjects that are often not found in our biographies or social environment. Thus, we crave to overcome the boundaries of our social and spiritual world and try to get in contact with the totally Other. Analytical psychology of C.G. Jung refers to the Self in this context, as a center of personal being that influences goals beyond our conscious realm. The self creates scenarios and sets goals without us being aware of them. We are therefore not only objects of our fate or the pawn of circumstances but also unconsciously manipulate our environment, choose influences, and shape relationships to realize our inherent life scheme. From a medical and scientific perspective, these could be understood as genetic structures that are activated in specific contexts or in the face of external challenges. These genetic patterns outline our scope of experience. We therefore tend to behave in ways that cannot be explained as the result of external influences, upbringings, or social expectations. We perceive them as a striving for goals, experiences, and interests outside our social milieu. We are confronted with desires and ambitions that cannot be derived from our environment.[6] With children and adolescents, these aspirations might express themselves in imagined figures. They rave about characters that are distinct from their lives and their milieu. Younger children enthuse about the Indian boy Jakari or Paw Patrol or other comic figures. Pippi Langstupf remains a star with older children and, of course, the games on the internet feature heroes, villains, and adventurers with whom one can identify. In *Game of Thrones*, thousands of young people immerse themselves in the medieval fantasy world of Westeros and Essos. They are enthusiastic about figures and challenges that they neither encounter in school nor at home. They do not correspond to their current lives. The internet allows them to identify with figures which they don't encounter in their personal lives. They dream of becoming YouTube celebrities, football stars, tennis stars, successful influencers, or famous musicians. They fantasize about them, even though they know that it is very unlikely that they will ever assume the same role. Mentally, they follow surreal models. However, the infatuation for these characters and actions expresses a striving for otherness and often stands out from milieu prejudices and biographical restrictions. They transcend their own existence and transport themselves mentally into another world. Children or adolescents set goals for themselves that are beyond their surroundings.[7] Especially during adolescence, they scan their surroundings for figures that signal escape. In the past, these were ideas attributed to the liberation fighter Che Guevara. He was a romantic projection figure and symbolized autonomy and rebellion. These fantasies of escape express an urge for self-realization.

Young people often strive for goals outside official curricula and hope for a life that supersedes their existence. Often, they identify this realization with forbidden activities. What is not allowed promises otherness, be it smoking pot, intense gaming, or violence.[8] In Jungian terminology, the influence of unconscious collective guidelines on the individual psyche is described by the term archetypes. These are unconsciously imposing "behavioral templates," "structural elements of the soul that present themselves to us in the respective cultural disguise." We can understand them as soul determinants that influence us in addition to our personal imprints.

Archetypes are characterized by polarities. They exercise their power over us through symbols. The result is that their meaning can only be comprehended indirectly. For their appearance, archetypes choose cultural forms. What a culture develops in terms of figures, stories, and images is given an additional quality by these soul determinants. These objects and images thus influence our psycho-emotionality and way of thinking. Our actions, feelings, and decisions are therefore not only a consequence of rational considerations but also of the archetypal drama to which we are exposed.

One example is the film industry. Hollywood is successful worldwide partly because many scriptwriters have been inspired and influenced by the archetypal psychology of Joseph Campbell[9] and his depiction of the hero's journey with its various phases and figures. Archetypal stories not only impress, because they address deep-rooted psychic structures, but they also free us from culturally imposed constraints. The perceptual and mental space expands when we fantasise ourselves into other worlds and times. We imagine rehearsing roles that we would not dare to act out in our lives. They might be banned by the culture we belong to and our self-consciousness. The imagined roles and scenes might express dormant archetypical forces, though. We discover these forces within ourselves through imagination. This might help to overcome challenges and problems. Motives and desires that are hidden, but have not been acknowledged, might help to overcome difficulties and give our lives another direction. This is a reason why we work with stories in mytho-drama. When children or young people experience setbacks, are depressed, agitated, truant at school, lose themselves in leisure activities or for some reason are full of hatred, they are often obsessed with their problems. Stories help them to detach themselves from their societal setting and fears. They might develop fantasies that transcend the bubble they are living in. Stories are a way to understand life and oneself in all its archetypal scope. One realizes that there is more to life than one's own environment suggests, and we believe that. Mythodrama tries to expand one's thinking range using stories and imagination as triggers. The child or young person is freed from internalized deterrents and can imagine the unusual. Fantasies increase creativity and the likelihood of finding solutions.

In Mythodrama, however, not only mythologies from ancient times or other people's lives are employed but also contemporary stories from films or literature. They must have a certain knack, relate unusual events, break cultural codes, and often have a semimystical character. In literature, these can be characters like Holden Caulfield in *The Catcher in the Rye*[10], *David Copperfield* (Charles Dickens), Captain Ahab in *Moby-Dick* (Herman Melville), or in films characters like James Dean in *Rebel Without a Cause*, Tyler Durden in *Fight Club*, Vito Corleone in *The Godfather*, Darth Vader in *Star Wars*, and Sissi in *Forever My Love*.

ENDNOTES

[1] J. Haidt, *The Happiness Hypothesis*, p. 69ff.

[2] T. Rose, *The End of Average. How to Succeed in a World that Values Sameness.*

[3] F.R. Schreiber, *The Many Faces of Sybil.*

[4] A. Miller, *The Drama of the Gifted Child.*

[5] A. Frances, *Saving Normal.*

[6] A. Guggenbühl, *Wer aus der Reihe tanzt, lebt intensiver. Mut zum persönlichen Skandal.*

[7] T. Suddendorf, *The Gap: the Science of What Separates Us From Other Animals.*

[8] A. Guggenbühl, *Die unheimliche Faszination der Gewalt.*

[9] J. Campbell, *The Hero with a Thousand Faces.*

[10] J.D. Salinger, *The Catcher in the Rye.*

2

Phase One: Preliminary Work: Staging the Community

Summary

Mythodramatic groups are a valuable way of helping children or young people activate their own resources when dealing with problems and challenges. Stories expand the thinking range, so it becomes easier to find solutions to problems. The group members have the chance to develop own ideas about how to help and support each other. This chapter describes the considerations, actions, and preparations that need to be thought of when starting a mythodramatic group. It points out the prejudices of parents, children, and young people towards psychotherapy, which one must be aware of when parents or children seem reluctant to join or cooperate. I describe how to introduce oneself as a group psychotherapist to parents and the public, how to explain one's own work to laypeople, and how to establish contact with third parties. The role of diagnoses and assessment reports is critically reviewed. I discuss what conclusions can be drawn from diagnoses and reports, and what their significance is for group work. Finally, the procedure for preliminary talks with children and parents is explained, and the first phase of a mythodramatic session is described in detail.

New ideas usually don't emerge when we are desperately seeking answers, straining our mind, and focused on a computer screen. They come to us as a reaction to an unusual observation or an extraordinary event. We experience something that irritates us, astonishes us, or does not fit into our own way of thinking. We instinctively exert ourselves and mobilise hidden mental resources. We look for answers beyond our usual mental boundaries. This is what happened to me with Mythodrama. The idea to develop a group therapy in which one works with stories arose after I heard from colleagues, psychotherapists, child psychiatrists, teachers, educational counsellors, social workers and school psychologists that many children or adolescents are not willing to get help despite personal difficulties. They suffer because of family problems or difficulties at school, or they must deal with trauma or difficult developmental steps, but there is not much that can be done. Also, it was agreed, that school psychology services and educational counselling centres could not provide help because they had not the capacity to address the individual problems of these children or young people. Some services pointed out that individual therapy was not part of their job description and not covered by health insurance or the state. The functions of school psychologists in general include mental health interventions, behaviour management, crisis intervention and response, assessment, and consultation and collaboration. Giving advice and maybe executing behavior programs like cognitive behavior therapy was their approach. They have to fulfill an educational mandate and therefore could not deal with the deeper psychological issues. My impression was that they had to concentrate on behaviour management and had to exclude unconscious motives and imagination. Their core job was helping children or young people adapt. Often teachers and parents, though, complained that they did not receive any "real" help. They received elaborate reports, conclusions from assessments, and diagnoses for pupils they transferred to the psychological or psychiatric services. These wordy reports often landed in a drawer and had little effect. Social workers mentioned that they could not take care of children's or adolescents' individual problems or issues on a deeper level because the number of one-to-one sessions they could provide was limited.

Not that there is no need for their services. Many parents, children and young people are struggling and confronted with challenges that they cannot overcome themselves. They do not know what to do. Parents experience their sons or daughters being bullied at school, they are worried about their son's or daughter's internet use, fear bad influence from peers, or worry about the effects of family difficulties. My colleagues perceive an urgent need for support from parents as well as from children and young people.

Accepting help: A sign of weakness?

On the other hand, accepting help is delicate. Many people, parents as well as children, hesitate to seek help. Admitting the need for support is not easy. One would prefer to solve the problem by oneself. Not only because one does not want to feel dependent or at the mercy of a social authority, receiving help is also often perceived as a sign of weakness. Especially the members of the male gender feel their self-esteem is impaired when they must admit that they are not able to cope adequately and are vulnerable. They feel ashamed of not being in control of their lives. In their view, one accepts help only in extreme emergencies. For this reason, the psychological-psychiatric apparatus scares off many parents and children. "I don't want to have anything to do with psychiatrists, psychologists, or even a state child protection agency like the KESP in Switzerland (Kinder und Erwachsenenschutzbehörde)! My son is not disturbed!" is a widespread objection. Of course, my professional colleagues and I emphasize that accepting help is not a sign of weakness or proof that one is disturbed. Seeing a psychologist or psychiatrist doesn't mean there's a "screw loose" in one's head. Seeking support is normal. The objection is heard, but it often rebounds. Only weaklings and sissies get dependent on a psychologist or psychiatrist, according to the opinion of a part of the population. Help is accepted after accidents, but otherwise, people prefer to muddle through somehow. People don't want to be labeled.

The fear of losing one's power

However, the skepticism of many parents, children and adolescents is not simply due to insufficient information but also an expression of fears that must be taken seriously: People do not want to enter a relationship that puts them in a weak position. When someone turns to an official or specialized state agency, he or she loses independence. He or she becomes a case. As such, he or she must meet the expectations of the professionals.

If the costs are taken over by health insurance or the state, affected persons fear being obliged to be grateful or not being able to express criticism. This assumption is based on a widespread image: If you are healthy, you act autonomously. Being healthy means deciding for oneself what to do with one's life. This attitude is not only understandable but also is the foundation of a liberal society, in which people take their lives into their own hands and want to solve problems on their own.

For these people, accepting help means admitting that something is wrong. The fear is that a personal deficit or a dysfunctional family situation will be presumed. This is not only the case for parents, but also for children and adolescents. Adolescents also often experience support as an attempt by adults to rob them of their autonomy and determine how they should behave. Psychologists, psychiatrists, and social workers are then perceived as the extended arm of parents and the school.

The third element: The fearless knight

An answer to these handicaps in therapeutic work and counselling was initially hinted to me a few years ago by an incident with my then-5-year-old son. He was afraid to go to kindergarten alone. The kindergarten was easily accessible via a dirt road and completely safe from an adult point of view. Despite good coaxing from me and his older sister, he refused to make one step. We tried to convince him that no one was lurking around, that he would get a present if he walked alone, and that the kindergarten teacher, whom he liked very much, was waiting for him with a surprise. All these arguments were of no use; defiantly, he remained in his place. And then something unexpected happened: Suddenly his features brightened, and without a second glance, he walked along the path without the slightest sign of fear. What had happened? The boy later informed me, "It's simple, I'm a knight after all!"

The evening before I had told him a story about brave knights. The story had a strong impact on him. He spontaneously identified with the knight. The story gave him a template to overcome his fear and walk the path on his own — just like a knight. I drew two conclusions. First, children or adolescents can be helped by using stories because a third element or power is introduced. It is not an adult who generates a solution in a conversation, but the answer is derived from the story by the child or adolescent himself or herself. Also the problem was not followed by long explanations, presumed causes and related in an educational tone, but rather presented in an imaginal frame.

Stories thus expand the thinking space and support the self-search for answers. As I explained in the previous chapter, stories are part of human existence. The second conclusion was that when children or adolescents listen to and process stories that are relevant to all of them, they might be able to help each other. Their autonomy, which is very important to children and especially adolescents, is preserved. Adults live in a different world, have a different language, and are in the eyes of children and young people all too powerful. They dominate. In contrast, in contact with their peers, they experience a space of their own and often have the feeling of immediate mutual understanding. Exchange with children or young people of the same age group mobilizes energies. The feeling develops that one is not alone, but faces similar problems or challenges.

Group size: The diversity makes the difference

In Mythodrama, sessions follow a predetermined sequence, but what happens during the different phases is decided by the participants. The story serves as a stimulus and does not present solutions. Mythodrama thus provides a free space for participants to make their own contributions.

The group size in Mythodrama is six to 10 participants. This number is larger than in some other forms of group therapy. Therapy groups usually consist of no more than six children. According to Aichinger[1], experience has shown that with more children, it becomes difficult to control the group. There is a risk of chaos or unrest. Everyone who has led Mythodrama groups knows this problem: Some children don't want to listen to the story or run around; teenagers make stupid remarks or provoke. In Mythodrama, however, restlessness and resistance are understood as signs that the children or young people are beginning to be themselves. They do not conform to the adults but dare to express their own desires, fantasies, and aggressions. They open up and talk about topics that they otherwise conceal from adults. They are, so to speak, "among themselves." They focus on the other group members while the group leader fades into the background. Mythodrama also works with larger groups because it is more likely that the behaviors that become a problem at school or at home are reproduced. It is less likely that the children or adolescents hold back their issues and behave. The group leader witnesses their problems and emotions.

Mutual interests

The stories are chosen so they reflect the challenges of the group participants. For this reason, we work with thematic groups: The group members then share a suffering, conflict, or challenge. Mythodrama groups exist on the topics of divorce or separation of parents, psychological problems of a parent (Baldur groups), identity (girls groups), social skills, violence (bad boys group), children from alcohol-affected families, and boys groups. The children or young people know that they share similar experiences. For example, in a divorce group, their reactions to their parents' divorce are a topic, and in the group consisting of "bad boys," their crashes and violent incidents might be a common issue. The participants' problems are addressed indirectly in the stories. They encourage the participants to reflect about themselves and help them to open. They are meant to inspire or irritate the participants. The group members devote themselves to a story before they begin to talk about themselves.

Preparations

Mythodramatic groups are offered by private practices, school psychological services, educational counseling centers, foster homes, church youth services, state social services, church social services, child and adolescent psychiatric polyclinics, social workers working in school, or as part of family counseling. However, especially in rural areas, it is not easy to find enough children to form a group. It is therefore advisable to cooperate with other specialized agencies and jointly draw attention to the respective group. Spreading the information about the possibility of joining a group widely with flyers and mails usually does not lead to the desired success. According to my experience, one should spare neither time nor effort to personally contact colleagues who are likely to be interested and effectively refer children or adolescents. There is no point in regularly covering the whole team of an educational center with brochures and holding lectures about Mythodrama at team meetings if only one or two colleagues support Mythodrama. It is more promising to maintain contact with these two colleagues, who support and value group work.

The inclusion of preliminary information

To start a group, 10 to 12 registrations are necessary.[2] Since one must expect cancellations, it is recommended to overbook the group. The most important criterion for acceptance into a group is the child's or adolescent's ability to engage in social situations. Contraindications are children with a massive aggression problem or autistic spectrum disorder. When a group has enough applications, the preparation phase begins: The Mythodrama leader finds out about the situation and challenges of the children or adolescents who will join his group. He obtains information through interviews and written reports.

If available, the Mythodrama leader requests school, medical, or psychiatric reports. The goal is to get a picture of the children's or adolescents' lives. Of course, this requires the consent of the parents or the adolescents if they are older than 18. Understanding the reports received is not always easy. Psychiatric reports often contain a lot of information about background, the main and differential diagnosis, test results, and anamnestic information, but they are usually not focused on the concerns of group therapy. In some cases, they are written in psychiatric jargon behind which the personality of the child or adolescent disappears. For example, if the report states that a boy is prone to "affect incontinence" but is "otherwise tolerable in school," one does not yet have a real under-standing of his behaviour. What is going on at school or in the family? Does he sit motionless at the desk during school hours and not dare to speak?

Or does he snap, suddenly rise, and storm out of the classroom? As a group leader, you are interested in precise, subjective descriptions of behaviour and information about the social context.

The need for public relations work

In addition to collegial cooperation, however, promotional activities are paramount. Group leaders should blow their own trumpet, make their work known. The goal is that parents, school administrators, teachers, but also authorities, politicians, and media representatives should realize that the group program exists. Public relations consist of informative events, media appearances, visits to other institutions, a webpage, a presence on social media, and occasional articles. In my experience, psychologists and social services shy away from public relations. They are reluctant to expose themselves, afraid of criticism, shy away from the additional workload, and believe that the quality of their own work and word-of-mouth are sufficient. This certainly might be the case but often is not. It is therefore the responsibility of the group leader to attract some interest in what he is offering.

In Switzerland, Germany, and Austria, but also in many other European countries, group psychotherapy is supported by the state, paid by insurance companies, and maybe funded by benevolent societies. The representatives of these institutions are flooded, though, with leaflets, mail, and often have little time to clarify the relevance of a service. Therefore, it is necessary to draw their attention to one's own work, even it means being outspoken and persistent. If a profession does not stand up for its service, it risks disappearing from the scene. However, public relations are also important to reach parents and schools. Through information brochures, presentations, and personal contacts, parents, colleagues, other specialized agencies, and teachers realize that the groups exist. Of course, flyers describing the specific registration procedure, a professional website, and, above all, personal contacts are also of prime importance.

Institutions and professional associations have their blind spots. They tend to see patients, clients, or customers from the viewpoint of their professional backgrounds. They analyse behaviours and problems according to the guidelines of their profession and the discourse that prevails in their institutions. What is considered a problem among their colleagues is applied to their own cases. For example, if sexual molesting is an issue, then there is a risk than one concentrates on the accompanying signs, sees them everywhere and does not consider alternative explanations. These corresponding thought templates become solidified in team meetings, breakout talks, in ongoing training, and in professional journals. Patient histories are scanned for sexual molestation and gender inequities, and incidents are analysed with the help of these internalised precepts. Thanks to such a focus, misbehaviour is identified, but at the same time, there is a risk that normal behaviour is pathologised or false diagnoses are made. It can lead to inadequate pathologising or exaggeration of dangers. When kindergartners show interest in each other's private parts, sexual harassment is suspected, and therapy decreed. In the past, this behaviour was understood as an expression of normalcy. Psychologists and psychiatrists are influenced by the zeitgeist and diagnose according to diagnostic trends. For these reasons, one should examine reports of specialized places carefully despite a collegial relationship or other considerations. The group leader must therefore make it his or her task to read concrete incidents out of reports and narrations of reference persons. To get started with group therapy, we need to get a clear picture why a child or adolescent should be treated. Questions should be asked. Why is a young person found to have "partially disruptive behaviour" or "lack of conflict competence"? What specifically did he or she do?

Concrete examples lead further

So when talking to colleagues about candidates or studying written enrollments, the group leader tries to detect primary impressions and specific incidents. His or her task is to get a picture of the child's or adolescent's personality based on observations. This often manifests itself in examples of the child's or adolescent's behaviour. If a teacher describes a boy who is "tremendously naughty," then it is important to find out more about him: How was he naughty? What behaviour led to this conclusion?

The group leader tries to reconstruct incidents and problematic behavior by recounting them in his or her own words. He or she tries to find out in what context the child or adolescent misbehaved or was conspicuous. If the teacher reports that he or she called her "bitch" after he or she had to apologize for an inappropriate remark during a game of football, then you have a clue for therapeutic work. Maybe the boy loses his temper when he is engaged in a game where he must prove himself. This could be a sign of ambition. In addition, the group leader should keep this in mind: The student in question will also remember this incident, and it is very likely that it still preoccupies him or her.

Well-intentioned is not always good: clarification odyssey

Some children or adolescents who are registered for the group have been through an odyssey of examinations. They had interviews with psychologists, curative educators, psychiatrists, and social workers, which are documented in a mountain of files. These bear witness to efforts to understand and help the child or adolescent in question. However, they are also indicative of the pressures to which he or she was subjected. The reports testify to a long history of disruptive behaviour and often are indications of a deeper psychological problem. Often it's revealing to hear the explanations or versions of incident by culpable children or adolescents.

Two examples: A boy systematically disobeyed teachers' instructions. He himself did not see this as a problem but proudly told me that he was the only one in school who had never, ever done any homework! He felt he was a hero! A girl habitually skipped school and drove her single mother crazy with her aggressive behaviour. If the mother did not parry, the daughter threatened to lock her in the storage room or *glory hole* during the day. In a conversation with me, the daughter put this threat into perspective: It had only happened twice, and she had really had to lock her mother up because her behavior was inappropriate according to her.

The goal of these investigations is to find background and reasons for the misbehavior. It is not normal not to be normal. Permanent norm violations might have psychological, social, medical, or neurological causes. In many cases, the behaviour is a result of dysfunctional or psychological complicated family situations; in other cases, certain personality traits, personal emotional troubles, or personal histories lead to problems. The hope is that these children or adolescents will calm down, feel better, gain self-confidence, and finally behave appropriately after we uncover and work on the causes. We look for clues as to what went wrong in the development, in the social environment, in the support, and led to a deficit.

In psychotherapy and psychiatry, deviant behaviour, deficits, and emotional problems are not expressed flatly and unfiltered, but by referring to professional language codes. We tag the norm deviations and deficits with the help of the category system of our profession and try to deliver a differentiated assessment. In psychotherapy and psychiatry, we use the ICD-10 diagnostic system of the World Health Organization (WHO). We identify cognitive deficits, mental abnormalities, psychosocial impairments, affective disorders, perceptual deficits, and many more abnormalities. The symptomatology is based on clinical experience and scientific research. Mostly, however, it is a descriptive diagnosis. In other words, they are based on precise observations and set-up experiences.

The advantage of this category system is that this is exchanged, shared, and thus knowledge is disseminated. Diagnoses are compared, questioned, and new diagnoses, such as toxic masculinity, are proposed. Efforts are made to be objective and professional in order to initiate discussions about conspicuous behaviors or conditions. However, we must not disregard the fact that observations depend on cultural prescriptions and current conceptions of illness.[3] Diagnoses reflect the level of know-ledge of the professional state at the time.

However, often the findings do not correspond to our experiences with the child or adolescent in question. Sometimes the child's or adolescent's behavior in the group is even diametrically disparate to the diagnostic findings. One boy was diagnosed with hyperactivity. In the group, however, he behaved calmly and even seemed adynamic to us and the other children. Another boy was diagnosed with autistic traits and contact problems, but in the group sessions he was approachable and established excellent contact with the other group members. Such recurring experiences made us skeptical of the claims of these reports. We consider them valuable but not always accurate.

The disparate impressions and conclusions are due to some children's and teenagers' capability to draw quite different behavioural registers. If need be, they behave intimidated and taciturn; in another situation, they switch and seem open and outspoken. In addition, most reports only marginally capture the real-life experience of the respective child or adolescent. Also, and astonishingly, one hears little about the child's or adolescent's views and his or her perceptions. In the case of behavioural and mental health problems, it is also important to take this subjective internal view into account[4], because each person feels, shapes, and verbalizes his or her problems differently, expresses them often with the help of very personal images, and sets independent contexts.

The harmful effects of diagnoses

The danger with too comprehensive assessments is collateral damage. Children or adolescents are tested, interviews are conducted, and meetings are held. The attention they get and the feedback they receive from the adults leave traces. The more effort that is made because of them, the more often they see a psychiatrist, psychologist, or social worker, the greater the risk that they are convinced they are not normal. Some begin to suffer under low self-esteem, others become cynical or intimidated. Over time, they become convinced: I am a deficit creature. Not every child or adolescent has enough resilience to put this perceived or real message into perspective. Of course, it is not the intention of the psychological or psychiatric services to intimidate. What is underestimated, though, is the strong impression judgments from outside authorities might have. For many, the assessment is the very first feedback of the world "out there" on their personality — something which they will not forget. The danger is that already the diagnostic procedure is perceived as proof that they are disturbed, that there is something wrong with them. When they hear that they suffer from attention deficit hyperactivity disorder (ADHD), show autistic symptoms, or that their social behavior is unusual, this affects their personality. "Something is wrong with me, and I have to change," they hear, or else: "I am disturbed, I can get away with anything!" The consequence: They behave in all further conversations with professionals as it is apparently expected from them, and even adapt to the jargon and demeanor a disturbed child or adolescent demonstrates.

Intelligent children or adolescents realize that language serves not only to communicate content but also to conceal unpleasant facts. Just as the speech of adults must be deciphered, they themselves say something, but what they really think is another story. The diagnoses seem to have a self-fulfilling prophecy. Not everyone reacts dejectedly, however. Many begin to adjust to their diagnosis. "You know, there's something wrong with me in my head, my brain doesn't work right, that's why I act weird," one 13-year-old boy informed me when I first met him, and a teenager I saw was firmly convinced that he couldn't empathize with his peers because he was autistic. The psychiatric explanations were internalized and served as an excuse for inappropriate behavior. One 16-year-old girl explained to me that she skipped school and smoked pot excessively because she had suffered trauma prior to adoption. The child or adolescent attributes his or her disruptive, problematic behavior to childhood events, neurological deficits, or psycho-social ills. The group visit then becomes, from the point of view of these affected children and adolescents, a measure to "patch them up." Their personality is to be changed. From a psychotherapeutic point of view, this is problematic and a poor way to start psychotherapy.

Prejudices and attributions reflect the social context

Often, however, outside information or reports are limited to observations and behaviour descriptions. School reports seldom contain information about what conclusions the child or adolescent draws by himself or herself. Insights into his or her inner world and subjective views of the conflict are rarely included in reports. They take the perspective of an onlooker. What the child or adolescent does is paraphrased, often without any con-siderations for the personal background. It states that the student ignores instructions, ostracizes classmates, isolates himself or herself, fails in class, uses drugs, provokes teachers, refuses to perform at school, skips class, or reacts violently in conflicts. It is understandable that the descriptions remain on the surface. Teachers are not explicitly asked to explore the background of a behaviour because their task is teaching. Furthermore, many teachers deal with more than 60 students in different classes during the week. They have neither the time nor the knowledge to delve more deeply into the individual student. They must protect themselves against getting too involved in the fate and situations of students because that might distract them from their main task: educating young people.

Reports from social or school agencies therefore usually don't provide in-depth information about the emotional and psychological condition of the child or adolescent. The problem is also that many children or adolescents mask themselves at meetings. When they are facing a grown-up professional who asks them questions and wants them to fill out a test, they naturally hide feelings and answers to personal topics. This is not a conscious decision but an instinctual reaction to the setting of the interviews in some school agencies. Many children or adolescents keep a low profile in front these agencies because of a lack of trust and because they want to protect themselves. Some children or adolescents even feel threatened. To divulge secrets to an unfamiliar person seems risky to them. You never know if he or she will exploit the information you give. Therefore, it seems logical that teachers and social workers often are unable to obtain in-depth information. Furthermore, the structured procedures of the interviews make it difficult to find out what is going on inside a student. Also, most children and adolescents do not have the capacity for deep reflection. They act out their problems without a lot of thinking. Despite these shortcomings, school reports are a valuable resource for group work because they often contain descriptions of how a child or adolescent behaves in a social environment. While we might not know what is going on inside the child or adolescent, what his or her fantasies, desires, and expectations are, we can imagine the impression the child or adolescent makes in his or her social setting.

The reports of files

Family members or other related persons should also be questioned. Since they are immediate relatives, their accounts are not always objective. They might contain prejudices, unrealistic expectations, hopes, projections, and tend to retell intrafamily narratives. Delicate issues and taboos might be avoided. One hears what fits the self-image of the family and can relate to an outsider of the family. Depending on the intrafamily dynamics, attributed traits and fabricated events come to the fore. In extreme cases, delusion are apparent. Parents impute personality traits to their son or daughter that are not apparent in extrafamilial contexts The father of a 10-year-old girl described to me how his daughter solved the most difficult intellectual riddles at home and mastered three languages with ease! According to him, she was highly gifted, and it was obvious that she is bound to be a professor someday, like everyone in the family! Her teachers disagreed. Meeting her and talking to her, it quickly became evident that the girl was a lovely, good-hearted and approachable girl, but her intelligence was below average. This assessment of mine did not suit the parents at all, as they were still convinced that their daughter was destined for an academic career, as is expected in their family. According to them, my judgment was evidence of my incompetence. Conversely, problematic or disagreeable traits are hidden in an attempt to mark normalcy. The impact of the son's smoking pot is discreetly overlooked, or the daughter's alcohol consumption is underestimated.

Information from immediate caregivers is important for psycho-therapeutic work. Parents know their sons or daughters well and place problematic characteristics in the context of the family. Typical family strengths and weaknesses are recognised. The rebellious behaviour of an adolescent loses its explosiveness when the successful and socially adapted father remembers that he himself was a troublemaker as an adolescent and had been expelled from school because of his behaviour. Often behavioural disorders are an expression of an unusual individuation path that is widespread within the family, such as: "All Barmettlers had problems at school, but later they become something proper!" The information from parents and other caregivers is one piece of the puzzle that must be put together to understand a client.

The opinions of children and young people are also important

Once the preliminary clarifications are completed and the reports studied, the group candidates are invited individually to a first meeting. The goal is to get to know the candidates individually but also to prepare them for the group sessions. Most children and adolescents have been enrolled in mythodramatic group therapy by their parents, their school, or agents in social services. Some children or adolescents found out about the group during story festivals, which they attended and were organized by us. However, most children or young people have no idea what to expect. They are not acquainted with group therapy. Understandably, some would rather spend their time differently. Some don't understand why they should spend Wednesday or Friday afternoons in a room with other children or young people and two adults. They fail to comprehend the purpose of group work, even though their parents or specialised agencies explained it to them. They prefer to spend their time with self-chosen activities.

Even after informing parents and social services personally about our work and on the homepage, in brochures, on the phone, and through other channels, one still can't be sure that children or young people realise what they are signing up for. For many, however, it does not matter what they know about group work at the start. If their mother, father or the friendly school psychologist suggests that a group visit would do them good, then they conclude that it's OK. They are ready to join because of the recommendation of a trusted caregiver. However, they do not know what they are getting into and what exactly Mythodrama is. Therefore, it cannot be assumed that the children or adolescents have an idea of what is going on during the sessions.

The context of the initial encounter also matters

After the preliminary information has been received, parents are invited to come with their son or daughter to the Mythodrama venue. The first contact with the child or young person usually happens in the waiting room. The quality of this initial contact is important and can leave a lasting impression on the child or adolescent. The group leader must try to connect with him or her. The way a child or adolescent is greeted influences his or her attitude toward the group. Does he or she feel welcome, patronised or ignored. Their very first impression sinks in and defines their attitude toward the group. The signals the group leader gives are therefore decisive for future group work. He or she should convince the respective child or adolescents that the group sessions are for their well-being and not to please parents, schools, or social services. For this reason, he or she greets the child or young person before addressing the parents or other accompanying persons. The group leader introduces himself or herself with his or her name and function, and asks the child or adolescent to follow him or her into the consultation room. The parents are informed about this procedure, though, beforehand. They realize why we approach the child or young person this way. According to my experience, this approach is accepted by parents, even if they are pressed to have a talk with a group leader and pass on the latest developments. The purpose of this procedure is to upgrade the children or adolescents. They realize it is about them, and their contribution is excepted. The group leader then has a talk with the child without the parents being present.

Greetings signal meanings

Most of the children feel they are appreciated and follow me willingly and contently into my consulting room. Many were delighted, others slightly surprised, and only a very few younger ones turned to their mother or father to obtain his or her approval or comfort. In the consulting room, I usually start with small talk, picking up any topic which is in the air, before asking him or her why they are here, why they have been registered for the group. Their answers vary. Some shrug their shoulders, avoid eye contact, and affirm that they have no idea why they need to come to me. Others claim that their mother or the school forced them to come and remain vague about the reasons. A fair number relate the reasons quite accurately. Sometimes children start a performance. They want to impress me, but more importantly themselves. They brag about their careers as truants or troublemakers, describe their misdeeds with a proud undertone, or complain about envious colleagues. Some tell me that they don't need any help and certainly don't need to consult with a psychologist. As mentioned, it happens again and again that young people inform me shamefaced that "something is wrong" with them. They claim their "brain is not functioning the way it should," that are just "not made for school" or believe "something went wrong at birth." Some present themselves as heroes. They see in their deficit a sign of honor and proof that they are special: "Anyone who doesn't have an ADHD diagnosis is a bore." A guy revealed to me. Other teenagers, however, feel miserable and have a low self-confidence. They think they "suck." Now and then I carefully share with them, what I have heard and read about them, without being judgmental.

Course of the preliminary interviews

The content of the preliminary talks is of minor importance. The goal is to communicate so one can get to know the child or adolescent. I try to figure out his or her mindset, hear out his or her views on current issues, school, and finally I am curious to hear his or her explanation for being sent to me. Most of the children or adolescents retell what has been told. The voices of the parents or teachers speak through them. If they are motivated to enroll in a group is at that point often not clear. It does not really matter, though. Children and adolescents are in a stage of life where adaption is paramount. Also, it must be considered that children especially have difficulty reflecting about themselves and their own behaviour in a differentiated way. They lack words and often the ability to problematize their own feelings, reactions, or goals. Children especially are not used to distinguishing their own personal part in a problem. For these, it is an indisputable fact that the teacher is unfair or a thick-head or mother simply does not understand that gaming is harmless. Children tend to evaluate events from their subjective, often egocentric point of view. They externalise their problems. Their descriptions seem authentic, yet it is difficult to discuss their experiences from a metaperspective. They hardly question their perceptions. What has to be considered, furthermore, is that these young people belong to a specific age group and therefore often talk a different language. The words they use are loaded with meanings we are ignorant of, and their perceptions of their lives and school differ. Their world is not the same as the world of their teachers or psychologists. The reasons by which the children or adolescents try to explain or excuse their behaviour or problems are often arbitrary or afterthoughts. Something happens, and then they try to find a cause. Often, we hear far-out explanations, which sound like lousy excuses. A student is convinced that he was excluded from class because he "only forgot a notebook" or the teacher has problems with her boyfriend. However, this developmental egocentricity does not mean that these children behave antisocially or lack a sense of community. The above student behaved impossibly in class, but at the same time, he lovingly presented his teacher with his own homemade drawing of an accident involving two Maseratis for her birthday. Despite this courtesy toward the teacher, he still lacked in insight that he should not call her "stupid cow" and leave the classroom in the midst of a lesson, swearing loudly.

In the preliminary meeting, the group leader explains how the group session's function, how they will be conducted and what is expected from the participants: They will hear stories, play games, and, above all, can interact with other children. We also mention that children and teenagers usually enjoy attending the group sessions. However, the group visit is voluntary. The first two group sessions serve as a taster, though. After having attended two sessions, they might be invited to join. They themselves can step back after these two sessions. In a certain way, we coerce them into the group. We allow them a personal impression, though, before we ask them to make their final decision. We make it clear, however, that not everyone will be accepted. A definite entry is only possible if the group leader has the impression that they fit into the group and are willing to participate! The latter is an important criterion for admission. In some groups, especially the bad boys, we inform the children or youngsters, that it depends on our impression whether they can join the group. They will have to wait until the second or third session. We then tell the participants whether the group is indicated for them. This is not just a trick; the group leaders make it clear that the choice is theirs and that we only work with participants who have personally decided to give it a try. One of the criteria for admission is the willingness to participate. Most of the children and adolescents are willing to join the group. They are more motivated, though, to give their best when they realise, that being part of the group is a privilege. We inform them consequently that regular attendance is expected.

The union of the rascals: The conditions to join the group

There is a reason for this approach: No one wants to join a group that is open to everyone, regardless of character, behaviour, and history. Such groups have no distinction code, and joining them does not increase one's personal value. In the view of many children and adolescents, such a group consists of losers. One can argue that when we are dealing with children and adolescents who are struggling with problems, experiencing family difficulties, and might suffer because of a trauma, such an approach is unethical. After all, we are dealing with people desperately in need of help. Setting admission criteria could be problematic. However, we have found that we must consider the goal of therapeutic sessions. Our experience is that children are more likely to engage in groups, and the chance of improvement increases when they attribute success to themselves. The admission test signals the children or adolescents that we do not perceive them as victims. We see them as individuals who are in charge. We appeal to their personal responsibility. Our message is: You can overcome your problems. After getting to know the candidates better, we inform them during the second or third session what our conclusion is. They were accepted when they made a good impression on us. That means they can join the group. Most of the children or adolescents feel upgraded and often react with exhilaration. They finally achieved something! This experience is important because many of them felt like "trash children" or "waste adolescents." Attending the group becomes a kind of initiation. Their lives are changing. For the few children or adolescents who are not admitted, we suggest other measures: individual therapy, a school-based program, or family therapy. We connect with agencies or colleagues that referred the child or adolescent and discuss with the parents and teachers how to find other solutions.

Beginning of the group: Subtopics of the individual sessions

After the interviews, a study of reports, and discussions with referring professionals or parents, the child or adolescent is invited to the first group session. Children receive a personal invitation, provided their parents agree. Adolescents naturally are addressed personally, too. If the child or adolescent joins an ongoing group, the group leader welcomes him or her at least 10 minutes before the group starts. When the session begins, he or she introduces the newcomer to the other participants. Usually, the leader then encourages the participants to report to the newcomer what they have been doing in the group, what their backgrounds are, and how they are working together. The newcomer can then add some words and introduce himself or herself. In contrast to the open groups, closed groups hold their sessions during a certain time and offer a restricted number of sessions, usually between 12 and 15. Closed groups are advisable for children and adolescents who need help coping with immediate challenges or changes in their lives, be it the divorce of their parents, difficulties at school, or being integrated. Groups to increase social skills last at least six months, and for crisis interventions in schools, we limit ourselves to four group sessions.

As mentioned, the groups focus on a theme that the children or adolescents share. In addition to parental divorce and social skills, it may be conflicts in the local community, behavioural problems at school, difficult parents (from the children's or adolescents' point of view), alcohol-involved family, abuse, etc. Thematic groups are more likely to be accepted by parents as well as by the children and adolescents. Compliance is more likely. Groups that are open to children or adolescents with any type of difficulties are met with more skepticism. It is easier for children or adolescents to join a group when they know before the first session begins what they are about and what topics they will share. Of course, this is only the tag the group carries. During the sessions, all themes of urgency can be discussed. How the common theme is presented and discussed is decided by the Mythodrama leader. He or she determines the subthemes of each session. He or she decides after consulting the group members, a personal assessment, or following the suggestions in the Mythodrama scripts. However, the groups are led in a *process-oriented* way. This means that the Mythodrama leader does not have to stick to the program described in the script. He is free to change the program. Only the sequence with the mythodramatic phases and the stories are fixed. The problems of the participants have priority. What is mentioned spontaneously during the sessions comes first. The goal of the sessions is individual answers and not the implementation of predefined solutions.

Nervousness and a rapt attention

The atmosphere during the first two to three sessions is usually constrained. When a group of strangers comes together and all realise that they soon they will be sharing intimate details of their lives, this creates a lot of expectations and fears. However, no one knows how his or her experiences will be. Dozens of questions run through the minds of participants as well as group leaders and parents present. The children hold back and often make a shy impression. They ask themselves: Will the others accept me? Might they think I'm stupid? Why do I have to join this group of "troubled" kids? Will I be liked? Meet friends? They harbor fears, struggle with anxieties, or are simply curious. With younger children, parents are invited to join at the beginning of the first group session. Naturally, they wish to get an impression of the group leaders and eye them with skeptical, expectant, or encouraging looks. They, too, are worried: Isn't the blond boy speeding around the room too aggressively? Is my son being exposed to bad influence? Why does the group leader wear wash-out jeans? Most of the questions and fears are *not* expressed. There are some exceptions, but people refrain from speaking their minds; instead, they put on a friendly face and wait for what comes.

During the first meeting, the group leader outlines the way one collaborates within the group and with the parents. It's important that he or she takes the lead in shaping the group. Therapeutic restraint is not appropriate. The leader signals by his or her demeanor to both parents and children that he or she is willing to take responsibility. This does come natural to every group leader. Many therapists prefer an introverted, harmony-oriented attitude, and refrain from making personal statements that might lead to misunderstandings or concerns. Therefore, at the beginning of a new group cycle, one must make an extra effort, overcome personal inhibitions and be ready to expose oneself without dominating the scene. The initial impression lays the foundation for the successive therapeutic work and influences the group climate.

Depending on how the group leader presents himself or herself and how confident he or she appears, the group will work together constructively or might be confronted with discord right from the start. The primary impression that the group leader leaves with the children or young people influences the course of the group. Will the sessions turn out to be chaotic, or is constructive cooperation possible? The calm that predominates during the first session and the attention rendered to the group leader is an opportunity to voice ideas of collaboration. Most children and youths perceive and are influenced by the group leader's attitude, mood, and mental state. According to Dan Zahavi[5], the initial impression is a kind of empathy, which is not disturbed by intersubjective processes. The group leader leaves an image of himself or herself that resonates with the children and youths. Each group has its own profile. The groups are as different as the people who compose them. Since, at the beginning of a cycle, one does not know how a group will turn out, one has to be prepared for anything. It could be that the group is difficult to manage and the children don't get along, or maybe the group will turn out to be supergood and enjoyable to lead.

Most children or young people wonder what role the group leader will take. Does he or she tend to withdraw into the background? Does he or she act like a teacher? Will he or she impose a program? Is he or she a slob? It is important that the group leader uses the vagueness and openness that prevails during the first two sessions to introduce himself or herself as a good-natured authority. The children and young people should notice that he or she is willing to take responsibility for what happens in the group, that he or she expects them to participate, but at the same time allows enough space for their ideas. The leader's performance is like an act in front of a skeptical theater audience. The group leader communicates how he or she envisions cooperation among the children or young people. The leader should be perceived as a person who is committed to an idea of group work and wants to realise it. He explains that he will tell stories and expect them to listen, but also play, draw, speak, and act.

To be convincing, he must try to connect with all the children, young people, or adults present and keep an eye on them during the session. Children especially should notice that he or she reacts when they are restless, absent-minded, irritated, or sad. Above all, the leader must assure the participants that he or she is *interested* in them and does care about them. However, his or her interest must not appear artificial or controlling. Children or adolescents react with resistance when the group leader puts on a forced, funny, overly empathetic, too authoritarian, or too distant demeanor. In contrast to adults, children and adolescents hardly hold back with their judgments when the group leader does not suit them. Especially when they feel protected by the presence of their colleagues, they can be rather blunt. After the third session at the latest, they express what they appreciate or dislike about the group leader. Their judgments can be harsh, might even hurt. In one group, for example, a slightly overweight group leader dressed up as the princess in the mythodramatic story. She wanted to surprise the children. "Such a fatty can't be a princess!" was the spontaneous reaction of some of the children. Children do not always notice the taboos that are mutually respected. They express what they think and feel.

Most children or young people wonder if the group leader has a genuine interest in them or is simply doing his or her job. As a group leader, you will have to be aware that you can't hide your feelings behind a facade. To begin with, the group leader does not disclose his or her personal feelings but does share his or her preferences and likings when it comes to the group activities. However, it is important that he or she points out his or her personal limits. The participants must realise what kind of behaviour is not acceptable and which rules must be followed: no violence, no assaults, no unexcused absences and — very important — the directives of the group leader must be respected! These no-gos should be communicated at the beginning of a group cycle, even when the participants appear obedient and peaceful. The group leader signals when he or she will intervene and which rules apply, but he or she also conveys that he or she is looking forward to the time together, will engage himself or herself, and is sure that they will have lots of fun. He or she indicates, though, that his engagement is not limitless. In return, the leader expects from them their commitment: They, too, should give their best. Of course, he or she is aware that this is only possible within the framework of the participants' personal resources and that many children have difficulties respecting the group rules. However, the point is that the children or adolescents should not be addressed as victims or as someone suffering from personality disorders but as capable of integrating themselves into the group.

If the children or young people are not attentive or are restless, as can be the case during crisis interventions in schools, the leader remains "cool." He or she doesn't beg for attention but instead waits patiently until the group calms down. He or she signals that the session will begin when all participants are ready, not a second earlier. The group members must adapt to the leader and not vice versa. This approach is more likely to be successful, especially in crisis interventions that are described to the participants, than when you implore them to be quiet and cooperate. This is not always easy. The group leader has to be determined to remain calm. He or she should not allow ambivalences to show.[6] If this does not work and the children or adolescents cannot be tamed, then the group leader might inform them that he is not willing to work with them under these conditions. However, according to my experience, this happens rarely. However, in order not to be at the mercy of the group, the group leader must be prepared to fail.

In many cases, this authoritative approach is not recommended. As mentioned, groups differ in their dynamics, responsiveness, cohesion, attention span, emotionality, and humour. Each group has its distinct profile. There are groups that remain peaceful and quiet, even in the second or third session, but in others, the participants talk and fool around continuously and seem to ignore the group leader, and others have the tendency to be chaotic. The mood depends not only on the constellation of the group but also on the topic and the assignment.

In crisis interventions, it is advised to be firm and decisive since, in contrast to ongoing groups, there is not enough time to relate to the children and adolescents and to resolve a conflict on a deeper level. The group leader must therefore try to install himself or herself as the head of a gang that initiates a process. However, individual greetings and personal questions are also important in crisis interventions. "Where are you from? Have you lived in this community for a long time?" or the like.

In thematic, ongoing groups, the focus at the start should not be on the declared problems, but it is important that the group leader uses the momentum to build up a relationship to the children or adolescents. This is important because children or adolescents usually do not know each other and are reluctant to share their personal feelings and issues. They have to gain trust in a group leader and among themselves in order to open up. At the beginning of the group sessions, the group leader should assert his or her determination to help the participants. If he or she gains the participants' trust, they are more likely to engage in the Mythodrama.

At the initial appearance, the group leader also emphasises that the sessions are minimally structured. Participants can decide for themselves how much they want to engage themselves, what personal experiences they want to share, and what they want to keep to themselves. The leader also points out the rules of etiquette that should be respected. They concern how to deal with each other and the topics that are discussed. The leader explains that Mythodrama is a method of working with stories. The participants will therefore hear a story in almost every session and are invited to continue it. The aim is to overcome personal inhibitions and confront challenges with the help of these stories. In the following chapters, the concrete procedures, principles, and psychology on which this approach is based will be explained.

The group is related to one's own life

For the group or individual participants to reflect on their behaviour, the group leader must point out the connection between the group members' activities and their personal issues. The participants should be aware that attending the group might result in changes in their school, family, leisure time, or themselves. The group will empower them to cope with their personal challenges. It is important to emphasize this because, unlike adults who are aware of the context when attending a therapy group, children or adolescents often confuse the group with reeducation, punishment, prescribed recreational activity, or a playgroup. They then tend to hold back, either because they are ashamed, they want to protect themselves, or because they do not trust the group and its leader.

Emphasizing the commonalities

The leader of the Mythodrama points out the shared interests of the participants. He tells them that they are facing similar challenges, are in a comparable situation, or are confronted with similar problems. He makes it clear that Mythodrama is a way to help them find their own solutions to their challenges. Therefore, during the sessions, the experiences of the individual group members have priority. However, the group leader guarantees that no one is forced to share his or her personal experiences or problems. They are allowed to hold back their deeper feelings and thoughts.

In the Baldur group, which is reserved for children with a parent who is struggling with a major mental health problem, it might sound something like this: "You all have dear parents, you like them. But: you've also had moments when you couldn't understand your mom or dad." He then gives examples of children from other groups or that he knows otherwise. For reasons of discretion, the examples are presented in a contorted way. So that the children can understand them and connect them to their lives, they must be described as vividly and explicitly as possible. In the Baldur group, for example, the Mythodrama leader describes how a girl's mother stormed out of the apartment at night in her pajamas and began singing religious hymns in the street; or how a boy's father crashed into other cars for fun while driving. When children or teens hear about the experiences of peers in similar situations, they find it easier to talk about their own experiences.

In the groups for children of divorce, the group leader explains that they all have parents who are separating or divorcing. He might mention some typical issues that children of divorce must deal with: two residences, difficult visitation rules, loyalties.

In social skills groups, the group leader will state that all group members feel overwhelmed in certain social situations. He might mention that their kin and teachers are worried about their behaviour and give examples to illustrate this. Other thematic groups are about identity problems, traumata's, stress in the family, or problems at school.

The Mythodrama leader emphasizes that the participants might have had similar experiences. Thus, the group members will focus on their social skills, the effects of their parents' divorce[7], acts of violence (the bad boys group), or the search for one's own identity (girls group).

Further topics were groups reserved for children or adolescents from families with alcohol problems, for children and adolescents traumatized by war (internally displaced persons [IDPs] or refugees), and for young perpetrators of violence. Mythodrama is an attempt to help participants find their own solutions to their problems. Therefore, during the sessions, the experiences of the individual group members have priority. However, as mentioned, no one is forced to share his or her personal experiences or problems.

Short stories do the trick

In one of the first sessions, the group leader might share what he or she knows about each participant. However, the leader emphasizes that he or she is merely reporting what he or she has heard or read. The leader leaves it open if it is true. It is important, however, that no one is not exposed. As a group leader, one needs to be careful not to shame or hurt a participant. One possibility is to create a small anecdote out of the information the group leader has received. The leader dramatizes the incident, behaviour, or situation he has heard of or read about. For example, if the leader read in a report that the youth pushed a desk from the second floor of his or her school building, the leader describes how he imagines the incident happened: the effort to lift the certainly heavy desk, the difficulty to shift it over the edge of the window, and finally the loud crash as it hit a sidewalk. Did a passerby applaud him or her? The group concentrates on incidents, and the leader restrains himself or herself from making statements about personality or diagnoses, and making categorical judgments. The respective child or adolescent is not bad-mouthed but presented as the protagonist of an extraordinary scene. We do not want to shame children but make it easier for them to talk about themselves, by referring to what they experienced. Morally reprehensible deeds are referred to as such but without devaluing the child or adolescent in question. "Suddenly you got angry, snapped at your colleague, and gave him your fist. Did you do it consciously? You know, even when you're angry, you don't hit right away." When describing incidents, the group leader refrains from using pronouns, such as "he 'is a troublesome student'" or "he 'suffers from an attention deficit disorder,'" but instead paraphrases behaviors.

The group leader decides on a case-by-case basis what preliminary information he can disclose. Also, he should consider when and where to relate the information: during a confidential one-on-one conversation with the child or adolescent or during a discussion with all participants. When the information is shared by all group members, it might produce the mutual feeling of being on the same boat. The children or adolescents realize that they are struggling with similar difficulties.

However, in the groups for children from alcohol-affected families, in the Baldur group, and in the divorce group, one must be careful in how one describes the significant others. Descriptions of their actions, events, and behaviours are usually unproblematic, but one should be cautious when it comes to background information. Not all group participants need to know that a boy's mother has attempted suicide twice or that a colleague blames him for being a traitor. However, actions for which children or young people themselves are responsible can be reported. Thus, the group leader may reveal to the group that a participant had threatened to set the school on fire or stole cell phones from a store, so he could increase his pocket money. The focus is on what the child or teen did.

In the ongoing group of violent juvenile offenders, the so-called "bad boys," the group leader confronts the youths about their deeds. "You apparently threatened a classmate. You stood in front of him and told him he was living dangerously! And then presented a knife!" he will state, for example. The boys hear the reasons that led to their enrollment in the group. As mentioned, the group leader refrains from moralising or talking in a disparaging tone.

Personal assessment: Behaviour within the group

Depending on the level of trust, the group leader may add a personal assessment. He or she then shares with the participants what the reports and conversations triggered in him or her. He or she tries to convey the perspective of other people. The leader uses phrases like: "That would annoy me as a teacher if a student . . ." or "I don't understand how some-one could do this to you." If it is a gross incident, such as an act of violence, cheating, or a racist action, he or she takes a stand after describing the incident: "Personally, I don't think you should push someone down the stairs just because they refuse to speak Swiss German"; or "I have nothing against alcohol, but I think coma drinking is disgusting!" The participants are unlikely to let go of their behaviour by such categorical statements, but in the long run it helps them to know where the group leader is standing. Often, he or she represents a moral counterpoint. The chance is that the child or adolescent will internalize the group leader's stance. The point of this phase of group work, however, is not to assign blame or pass judgment, but to convey the impressions of other people and authorities.

Except in cases of serious misconduct, the descriptions can be given in a humorous tone. Participants should be encouraged to reflect on themselves. This is easier if the mood is relaxed and the incident is not presented as grave misconduct. Humor transfers a behaviour or act to another level. One can smile without condoning or sanctioning the misbehavior. One boy had to attend the "social skills" group because his usurping behaviour has become a problem for his teachers. The group leader of the Mythodrama described an example:

"A hot summer day. However, the students of the fourth primary classes must write an exam. One boy is missing. After 10 minutes, the door flings open with a loud bang. The missing boy is standing under the doorstep, dressed in swimming trunks, diving goggles on his head and snorkel around his neck. He looks boldly at his schoolmates and shouts loudly, "So, I'm giving you all day off! We're going swimming!" The class roars, quite a few students stand up and sprint outside. The teacher has difficulty calming the boys and girls. The swamp-glasses boy is notorious for such actions, so he must attend the "social skills" groups."

The boy and the group, of course, realize that such behaviour cannot be encouraged by the teacher, although it's fun. The boy, along with his peers and colleagues, should consider what his intentions are when rehearsing such stunts and what the alternatives are. The incident is described dramatically and presented as a story to direct the focus to the psychological level. The goal is to get the kids to reflect on their behaviour.

Flexible objectives and expectations of mythodramatic therapy

When children or adolescents are enrolled in mythodramatic sessions, then everyone expects something to happen. The sessions are not about self-awareness but about coping with a distinct problem: a decrease in aggressive outbursts, more peaceful behaviour in the family, connecting with peers, reducing tension at school, coping with a gambling addiction, dealing with a difficult personal or family situation, and so on. Parents and professionals hope that attending the group will help the child or adolescent to deal with his or her problems. The children or adolescents are sent to the group with expectations. Parents and the school hope for a change in the behaviour, attitude, or emotional condition of the respective child or adolescent. As therapists, we do not accept the task forwarded by the parents or school unconditionally but discuss it on the basis of our own experience with the child or adolescent. Therefore, as a therapist, we make a definite decision about our focus after the second or third group session. The impression the child or adolescent leaves, the dynamics of the group in question, and whether the child or adolescent is motivated to engage in group work also play a role. Children or adolescents do not become different people by attending the group. The goal is to help them to cope with the causes of their problems or to enable them to deal with one side of their personality. The task of the Mythodrama leader at the beginning of a group cycle is to develop an idea on how the group sessions can help the child or adolescent in question and what specific goals can be targeted. The expectations and descriptions of their personalities from the environment are important, but often they do not correspond to the experiences of the group leader.

A 9-year-old girl was assigned to the social skills group. The girl was considered extremely shy and reserved. Apparently, she hardly ever said a word at school and refrained from getting in contact with her colleagues. Parents and teachers were worried about her. Selective mutism on the background of social phobia was the diagnosis she got by the psychiatric service. The hope was that she would lose her reticence toward her peers, dare to participate in conversations, and express feelings. In fact, she did remain silent during the first two group sessions and confirmed the diagnosis. She seemed to ignore both the group leader and the other children. In the third session, however, there was a breakthrough. She started talking — and then didn't stop! It turned out that she liked to boss others around and claim full attention for herself. Her mutism was an expression of an excessive need for control, not a social phobia. Group therapy uncovered the background of her mutism.

Because of such discrepancies between the impression in the group and the external perception, the objectives may change. Goals set by the school, parents, or other agencies are often conclusions drawn in a specific context. The child's behaviour might reflect the dynamics and norms of a particular social setting. In this respect, the social context influences behaviour. Disorders are often not only due to personality but also an expression of school or family constellations. Therefore, mythodramatic group therapy does not only focus on the diagnosed deficits but ventures into other settings if the experiences in the group impose this. If we were to stick rigidly to the orders of the outside authorities, we run the risk of closing ourselves off to unfamiliar sides and surprising characteristics of the children and adolescents. Purposefulness would thus become a defensive strategy against insights that emerge during the sessions.

ENDNOTES

[1] A. Aichinger, *Gruppentherapie mit Kindern.*

[2] S.R. Slavson & M. Schiffer, *Gruppenpsychotherapie mit Kindern*, p. 101ff.

[3] E. Waters, *Crazy Like Us. The Globalization of the American Psyche.*

[4] D. Hell, *Krankheit als seelische Herausforderung*, p. 20.

[5] D. Zahavi, *Self and Other. Exploring Subjectivity, Empathy and Shame.*

[6] Guggenbühl, A. Guggenbühl, Dem Dämon in die Augen schauen: Kriseninterventionen in der Schule. In M. Drilling & H. Wehrli (Hrsg.), *Gewalt in Schulen: Ursachen, Prävention, Intervention.*

[7] A. Guggenbühl, *Das Mythodrama. Eine Untersuchung über ein gruppentherapeutisches Verfahren bei Kindern aus Scheidungsfamilien.*

3

Phase Two:
Fun and Play

Summary

After the welcoming and conversing with the participants, the Mythodrama leader proposes an activity to the group. In this chapter, the importance of play is discussed, and what playful activities might trigger in the children or young people. Fun and play is a prepares the children and adolescents for the third phase of the Mythodrama: attending the story.

Playful encounters facilitate contact

"No! That I see you here again!"—the two girls race toward each other and subsequently hug each other and shriek with joy. They have finally met. Next to them are two boys. They greet each other as well. They pat each other on their shoulders. One says, "So, you survived it after all!" The other replies, "Looks like it!"

A few minutes before, the girls and the boys were standing around trying not to connect with another participant. They had been listening to the group leader's explanations for the last 10 minutes, refraining from group conversations. Within minutes the mood had completely changed. They talked with each other, fooled around, and had fun. Playful activity can help children or adolescents to open up. The game the group leader suggested led to a change in their mood! Joyfully, openly, and casually, they now approached each other. Their shyness had vanished.

First, the group leader invited the children to walk around the room to and fro and keep as much distance as possible from the others. A bit later they were allowed to exchange quick looks until, after further encounter variations, they were told to pretend that they met a very dear friend on the street by coincidence who had been missing for years. This exercise releases a lot of emotion and eases the mutual contacts among participants.

This and similar playful exercises are carried out in the second phase of the Mythodrama. The point is to loosen up the participants and prepare them for listening to the story. If the mood among the participants is restrained, such exercises will transform it. Thanks to such playful activities, children or young people who open up are more likely to express their feelings and are ready to approach each other.

Simplicity is the secret

There are countless games and social activities that can be done in this phase. The games or exercises must be adapted to the age of the participants and their interests. Younger children appreciate games that involve movement. Older children and adolescents prefer games that involve social interactions and are a bit "naughty." Games should be easy to explain, challenge participants, and, most importantly, be fun. Complicated games inhibit group dynamics. The games must also be adapted to the space available. Many exercises or games can only be carried out in large halls; others can be done in singing halls, conference rooms, or regular classrooms. If no room is available and the group is not too large, then social activities should be suggested that do not require much space. Exercises should also be chosen that do not require too much technical equipment.

The purpose of the activities is to relax the participants and get them into a playful mood. The goal is to enable participants to approach each other and express their emotions. They should experience themselves as a group. This makes it easier for them to concentrate on a story.

Playfulness is important throughout the session. In my experience, prompts to move, gesturing with arms, making faces, bobbing or jumping trigger a lot. Children, but often adolescents, get into a different mood. They put aside their restraint and experience themselves as well as the environment more openly. On the next pages, I will discuss what is meant by the mood change through playful activity. To understand this, it helps if we take a closer look at the attitude we are familiar with in everyday life and compare it with the playful attitude.

Normal submission makes us competent

Both behaviour and thinking depend on the social context and the social topography in which we move. As soon as children enter a classroom, their perceptions, thinking, and behaviors changes. The chairs and benches, the wall decorations, the teachers, and sayings on the walls signal expectations. The thinking and perceptions of children are influenced by what they see and hear. They talk and behave differently, compared to when they are amongst themselves or at home. This is natural because to move in a society, they adjust themselves spontaneously to the surroundings.

Adaption to the context requires a slightly detached attitude. The attention span, the gestures, and the facial expressions, as well as the reactivity and emotionality, vary according to the social context. At school, but also in public, children and adolescents are also expected to adopt a focused and calm attitude. That is the norm we follow unconsciously. This makes it possible for us all to comply with rules and codes. We have internalized the corresponding guidelines so that we can call them up automatically when we are in the corresponding situation. Our actions are goal oriented. When we enter a room, we routinely reach for the door latch, push the door open, and sit down in a chair. Small children, of course, are not accustomed yet to that mode. When they get a little older, they learn to refrain from small prances, to pick their nose, or run around.

Their behaviour tends to follow predetermined patterns and fulfill distinct functions. The environment sets the rules, which they abide. This also affects perception. The older children become, the more they can register what their collective or community is focusing on. They learn to register the signals for pedestrians, recognise crosswalks, but also slogans on the door, settlements, chairs, lamps, men, women, or roofs. The children's perception is calibrated according to patterns set by society.

In this way, children and adolescents acquire the competencies that are important in their social environment as they grow up. The older they get, the more their actions, as well as their perceptions, are purposeful. They move and do what their environment insinuates and are assumed to be capable of. They have internalized the codes, norms, and expectations of the environment. Their actions increasingly conform to social expectations: They flip a switch to turn on the light, put socks over their shoes with their hands, or smile when someone says something nice. They acquire the skills that are important to survive in their civilization. However, the concentrated-calm mode is not the only mode we dispose of.

The concentrated-calm mode differs from the playful mode. In this modus, one does not follow social guidelines, does not fulfill expectations and codes, but concentrates on the action itself. If we walk down the street on a sidewalk, then walking becomes the focus, and the purpose of our walk is secondary. One concentrates on the qualities and variations of walking, what we achieve with it becomes secondary. Variations of the step are considered pleasurable. One can tiptoe, wiggle a knee back and forth, take intermediate steps, hobble, walk backwards, stagger wide-legged, waddle like a duck, march like a soldier, lurch like an idler, hop like a ballerina, or stomp like a barbarian. If stepping on the sidewalk becomes a game, then the possibilities are endless, and we could ask the Ministry of Silly Walks for grant money. The problem: From a social perspective, such activities are useless. Except perhaps for John Cleese, no one can make a living from it.

In play, we are temporarily freed from explicit social obligations. The joy is evoked by the action. We don't need to fulfill a task or perform a certain service, but the activity itself becomes the goal. Playing means ignoring the implicit and explicit demands of the social environment. Neither one's tone of voice nor one's movements and gaze are oriented to the context. The meaning of play lies in the joyful activity. Play is a ubiquitous activity: not only walking down the sidewalk, but almost any purpose-oriented action can be performed playfully, such as closing a refrigerator, answering a question, putting on a jacket, and emptying a glass.

When a playful activity is called for in the second phase of Mytho-drama, the idea is to invite the participants to adopt a playful attitude. The younger a child is, the less this is a problem. Children spontaneously engage in the world through play, learning about themselves and their surroundings. Most children love to play and cultivate it intensively during their toddler years. As schoolchildren, however, they have to give up play more and more because of the demands of education and school; prudence, goal orientation, acquisition of competencies are the order of the day.

In the second phase of Mythodrama, the children's and adolescents' desire to play is evoked. They are asked to abandon the competence mode and to engage with their environment in a playful way again.

Play reveals our uniqueness

When we encounter the environment, other people, and ourselves in a playful way, this can trigger a lot in ourselves. The detachment from socially useful activities makes it possible to explore ourselves. The group participants register their emotions, notice deficits, experience their bodies, and perceive sensitivities. Because the activities serve no immediate purpose, participants become more aware of themselves.

Children and adolescents must adapt both at home and especially at school. The older they get, the less time they have for unplanned interludes such as spontaneously singing a song or fooling around. While adults calmly endure this imposed silence, frustration builds up in children. They have difficulty sitting still for long time, listening, or following a task in a disciplined manner. They feel the urge to be loud and move around. Therefore, play phases are immensely important in children's groups. Many children can forget themselves in play and have great fun.

Play also has a social meaning. The children and young people in the group can approach each other and get to know each other. As in dance, encounters with the other participants are deproblematised. The game determines who approaches and meets the other person and how. In the game "Communication with Hands," two group members face each other and communicate messages with their palms. They start with looking into each other's eyes; afterwards, they communicate blindly and finally in front of an unknown participant. This exercise draws everyone's attention to a form of encounter that is rarely noticed in everyday life. They experience the sensitivity of their palms.

The purpose of such games is to prepare the group participants for the next phase of Mythodrama: the story. At the end of the game phase, the children or young people are usually significantly more alert and receptive than they were during the greeting. This seems like a paradox, but sharing sounds, dancing, prancing to and fro, laughing, and engaging in seemingly purposeless play promote group cohesion and awareness. Thus, they are prepared for the next, quieter phase of Mythodrama, the story.

4

Phase Three:
The Power of Stories

Summary

Stories are the core element of Mythodrama. First, this chapter introduces the external conditions and the selection criteria of the stories and then describes the preparatory work. The stories that are chosen reflect the problems and concerns of the group participants and thus help them to find a language for their issues. They are written by the group leader accordingly or selected from a selection of stories. However, they also serve as a medium of contact. In Mythodrama, the chosen stories contain unfamiliar scenarios or might even irritate the listener. On the next pages, the reasons for this approach will be explained. Furthermore, the methods on how to gain the attention of the audience and to encourage them to participate will described. In Mythodrama, the participants are invited to profile the main characters and imagine the continuation of the story. In the second part of this chapter, I write about how stories are told and what guiding points a storyteller might want to follow.

The art of immersing oneself in another world

The look is stern, the tousled red beard is striking: the postman at the front door impresses Patrik. He is a tall and has a stern look. "I have mail for you!" he explains gruffly and opens his brown bag. Patrik had just opened the door of his cottage, when this impressive postman arrived. Patrik definitely did not expect someone to send him a letter out here in the sticks! Patrik scrutinized the postman and remarked on a tattoo that the postman had engraved on his forearm. "I have seen that tattoo before," Patrik thinks to himself. "The anchor and skull remind me of something.""Do you want this letter now?" the letter carrier hisses, holding out the letter to him. "Yes, I do," Patrik stammers, slightly intimidated. The letter is crumpled. Patrik wants to take it, makes a step forward. The man with the red beard smiles mischievously, waves one hand, while presenting the letter. He then leaves without saying a word. Patrik is puzzled. He tears open the envelope with his left finger, pulls out the letter, and studies the contents. He frowns as he is reading the lines. Suddenly, he expression changes, he smiles and mumbles: "So, so, should I really do this? . . . I am not sure if I am daring enough." Patrik scratches his head.

This is part of a story we tell children or adolescents in a mytho-dramatic therapy session. Before relating the story, the children or young people are asked to find a place where they feel comfortable. However, the requirement is that they are at least two arms' lengths away from their peer. The Mythodrama leader therefore asks them to spread out in the room. The young people usually lie on the floor. Some might lie on their backs, others on their stomachs, others casually lean against a wall, or hide themselves in a corner behind pillows. The attention of the young people varies, and there is always someone who tries to gain attention by faking a doze, making provocative remarks, or poking a colleague. Before the group leader begins the storytelling, he or she might dim the lights or draw the curtains of the room. Some group leaders accentuate the beginning of the story by lighting a candle or, for younger children, by ringing a bell. The children then grasp that a story is waiting for them. Children and even adolescents almost always look forward to hearing a story, even if their attention varies.

In Mythodrama, children or young people are presented with a story, which was specially selected to touch on the issues of the group. It reflects their challenges. However, the respective actions and scenarios do not explicitly cite the children's or adolescents' problems, but they present the issues in a disguised way. They are dealt with in *alternative topos*. Thus, the children or adolescents are not consciously aware that the story deals with their topics; they are tuned in to their issues on a deeper level.

The story is told right after everyone had the chance to play, move, jump, and fool around. The reason we choose this moment is that after having been active, most children or young people feel they need some quiet. The leader uses this momentum to introduce the story.

They must not disturb each other while listening to the story. If this happens anyway, the co-leader intervenes or the storyteller pauses.

The power of the spoken language

The leader tells the story by heart and in the language that is common among the children or young people, often in their dialect and by employing colloquialism. In other words, the leader speaks in a way that is customary among the children or adolescents rather than switching to standard English. In Switzerland, this is the dialect; in our Georgian groups, it is Georgian; and in Japan, my assistants spoke Japanese but needed the dialectal coloring used in Kyoto or Tokyo. In the U.S. (Northern California and New England), my assistants also addressed the children in their local tongue. Group leaders try to memorize the story beforehand by imagining each scene and creating a mind map. It is important that the storyteller does not put on an air, change his intonation or accent. He is also allowed to make grammatical errors or pronounce words incorrectly. Nobody speaks perfectly; in our spontaneous speech, we tend to make grammatical and pronunciation errors. Words are mispronounced, and terms are used incorrectly. We all use idioms. These linguistic irregularities should not be considered as a lack of linguistic competence or a problem. It would be inappropriate to abandon on one's own spontaneous speech and speak faultlessly, maybe to act as a role model for the children or young people. In Mythodrama, this is not necessary. Our linguistic deficiencies and peculiarities express our personality and background. It is easier for the children or young people to connect. Faulty expressions, slight speech errors, or slips of the tongue give our speech a personal coloration. If we mispronounce words, do not use terms correctly, and emphasize words in an unusual way, this will be perceived as a personal profile. The children or young people notice: The group leader are not robots, but human beings with emotions and complexes. Their idiolect makes them unique.

For these reasons, we do not use standard language in Mythodrama, and we will not read the stories off the page. Group leaders try to memorize the story beforehand by imagining each scene, connecting it to a personal experience, and creating a mind map. However, if the storyteller omits parts of the story, it is not always due to his forgetfulness. Perhaps the omission is for a reason. He or she realizes that something doesn't fit. Omissions and additions reflect the narrator's preferences and personality as well as the mood in the group.

Storytelling or the art to connect

We don't use the stories to educate them, draw their attention to a literary product, or impress; stories also serve as a medium to establish contact between the group leader and the children. An important side effect of the story is to convey the moods, feelings, and complexities of the storyteller to the children or young people. The leader reveals his emotions, his peculiarities, and preferences. This offers the children a valuable opportunity to relate to an adult, free from educational issues, age differences, educational goals, or rules. The chance is that this will lead to an encounter on a deeper level between the adult and the child or young person.

Communities depend on stories

Mythodrama relies on stories for another reason: Sharing stories binds groups together. When the participants concentrate on one voice, it triggers a centering effect. Tuning in to one person helps the group experience itself as one. All are focused on the group leader's voice, imagine themselves in the scenes he or she is describing, get mutually excited or amused. Stories bond in human communities.[1] Countries are knitted together with the help of stories of the past. Families cultivate bonding by creating photo albums or archiving films. Stories foster a sense of community and are the foundation of identities. With the help of stories, opposites are bridged, and emotions are shared.

Storytelling is also important for the group leader as a way to get in touch with the participants. When telling a story, the narrator naturally is at the center of attention. His tonality, depictions of the individual scenes, descriptions of the protagonists and the antagonists are listened to attentively by the children or young people. Because he tells the story by heart, he can observe the faces and immediate reactions of the children and young people. The narrator can respond to the facial expressions of the listeners by adjusting the story accordingly.

Irritations will lead us further

Children or young people are more likely to get interested in the story and are ready to imagine its continuation when the story fits certain criteria. It is important that the story is not educational. When the story relates an obvious educational message, many children or adolescents are dismayed. The reason is that they are accustomed to hearing stories with educational messages. In many children's books as well as in school, rules are conveyed about how to behave properly, what is good, and what is bad: One should be punctual, honest, not be mean or get angry, not steal or express schadenfreude. This is necessary. However, mythodramatic groups aim at something different. Their task is not to deliver messages that they have to abide to. The group leaders should not repeat what the children or young people already know, but their job is to indicate alternate ways of doing things.

The mythodramatic groups encourage the children or adolescents to rely on their own ideas and to search for solutions themselves. The stories enable the children or young people to look and think outside the box. Fiction helps them face dilemmas and challenges they could not confront in a straightforward manner.[2] The stories should therefore astonish the children or young people, start them thinking. This is the reason that the stories do not repeat familiar values and attitudes. They should encourage children and young people to find answers beyond their accustomed range of solutions.

Stories are particularly interesting for children and young people if they contain a surprising element. That is why we choose stories in Mythodrama that contain scenes that confuse. The listeners are puzzled and wonder what really happened. The stories can involve scenes that are not politically correct or interpolations that you don't understand at first. In the story above, the appearance of the man with the red beard is irritating. He behaves harshly and later in the story wants Patrik to choose another personality for himself and accompany him on a boat trip. Scenes can also be irritating; in another story, the protagonist is robbed and abandoned naked on a main road; in yet another story, an antagonist can turn his mouth into a slot into which floppy disks can be inserted. He can then see films that are projected through his eyes onto a wall. Irritations are scenes or references that cause astonishment, are morally reprehensible, or are in secret attractive.

Irritations are important because they stimulate reflection. If the story takes a course that one expects, the audience members remain in their habitual thinking patterns. They do not venture beyond their horizons. But when they hear something that astonishes, outrages, or appalls them, they react differently. They leave habitual thought patterns, become creative, maybe angry, and search for answers beyond the usual conclusions. A broadening of horizons occurs.[3]

The power of the archetypes

Another selection criterion is the topic. The story one presents should deal with an archetypal issue, a universal, innate image that derives from the collective unconscious or a pattern or knowledge that prefigures conscious behaviour.[4] So it's not about whether to spend the day on a sandy or stony beach but addressing a pattern of behaviour that is rooted in our unconscious. An archetypal theme focuses on challenges we master or fail at; it includes the objective and subjective. Such challenges might demand strategies that do not correspond with our conscious knowledge. To evaluate the archetypal quality of a story is important because societies tend to prefer particular patterns of action, while rejecting or even tabooing others. This might be the archetype of the victim, the hero, the son, daughter or fighter. Choosing an archetypal story helps expanding the scope of possible attitudes. The possible reactions are thus dispositions in our unconscious and might be activated in response to an external trigger. Archetypal challenges are motherhood and fatherhood, sibling relationship, love bonds, fighting off enemies, coping with hierarchies, with violence, jealousy, deceit, deception, farewell, hope, dreams. These are issues that preoccupy people irrespective of religion and nationality and are universally of great concern. At certain moments, we are envious of fellow human beings who are luckier than we; we get angry when someone cheats us, is not truthful, or is driven by an unrealistic expectation.

An archetype outlines a pattern for handling such challenges. For example, if someone threatens us with a gun and intends to rob us, there are different ways to react: One can pounce on the attacker, push him to the ground, and knock the gun out of his hand. We react as a hero, like Achilles in Greek mythology or Alexander the Great. Or maybe we begin to talk with the attacker, trying to distract him and divert his mind. We employ cleverness. This pattern is mirrored in the story of the Greek god Hermes deceiving Apollo or in the mythological figure of the trickster in the Winnebago.[5] Archetypes denote patterns of behaviour that recur throughout history. When we operate with archetypes in stories, there is a chance that we amplify the behaviour and experience of the child or young person by presenting historical, literary, or mythological material.[6] It is the cheeky and restless behaviour of a schoolboy we might detect in Achilles, Spartacus, Christopher Columbus, or William Tell. His behaviour is not just pathologized but seen as an entrance to imagination. We give his behaviour another language and grander scenery.

Opposites attract each other

Culture implies a lifestyle, common values, shared aesthetics, and convictions. However, culture is also what respective people create and generate. Cultures therefore tend to unify, while at the same time differences emerge. The quality of a culture depends on its ability to deal with the dilemma between uniformity and diversification.[7] For everything we say or do, there is also an opposite. What we want, fight for, or yearn for has a counter piece, is expressed in oppositions. We consider a person beautiful because we know hideous people. We describe someone as funny because we are also confronted with bores, and we are annoyed by our outburst of anger because we can also be calm. A quality or behaviour becomes comprehensible to us because we are also acquainted with the opposite: We speak of love because we know that there is also hate, we are impressed by someone's loyalty because unfortunately betrayal is also a reality. The discerned theme of a story should therefore be dealt with in a polar manner. This polarity can be expressed through the choice of protagonists or actions. If a sheriff appears, then we should also introduce a criminal. If a rich man enters the scene, then there ought to be a poor wretch around the corner.

Such contrasts create tension and arouse the interest of the listeners. They are asked to take a standpoint. In mythodramatic stories, we therefore make sure that opposites are dramatized. Many stories deal with clashes or showdowns. The narrator himself, however, does not take a stand and leaves it open as to what will prevail. Will the good guy win, or will the bad guy win? Will you achieve something by deception, or will honesty prevail? It is left up to the audience to take a position on what is better.

The reason for this design of the story is that children and young people tend to produce collectively accepted answers. They conform with what they think is expected and believe the narrator or their environment wants to hear. Shadow motives or problematic characteristics are elusive if the moral conveyed in the story vilifies such behaviour or motives. However, if behaviors and characteristics are portrayed neutrally, there is a chance that children and young people will reflect on their own shadow. In Mythodrama, we therefore avoid stories with a moral undertone and use stories in which the good, bad, problematic and wonderful qualities of people appear equally and given the same value.

Far away and yet close: the topos

A truism: We prefer to talk about other people's problems rather than our own. We gossip about a neighbour's stinginess, a brother-in-law's dopey opinions, or a colleague's marital problems, but we discreetly look past our own faults and weaknesses.[8] This is natural; otherwise, we run the risk of dismantling our self-image. We believe we belong to the good people. Often, we fail to see the faults of people close to us and the family. We blank out problematic behaviour that we observe in our immediate environment or family members. "Our daughter never lies!" proclaimed a mother of a 14-year-old girl furiously, after her daughter was caught red-handed shoplifting but vehemently denied it. We have great difficulty admitting actions or family secrets of which we are ashamed. We do not like to see our often idealised self-image crumble or our social position endangered.

The dilemma in therapies is that the patients prefer to talk about the misbehaviour of others rather than about themselves. However, therapies have to include the patients' part as well. Therefore, group therapy should be the place where people also address their dark personality traits and misdeeds. Accordingly, in mythodramatic groups, the problems that one is describing at the beginning of a cycle should be addressed.

The strategy in Mythodrama is that one's shadow is not directly addressed but packaged in a story. To prevent the listeners from blanking their shadow out, the sensitive topic is dealt with in a separate topos. For the presentation of a taboo or problematic feature, a setting or historical context is chosen that is unfamiliar to the audience. The story takes place in the favelas of Rio de Janeiro or is set in the Middle Ages. In this way, the listeners don't react immediately with aversion. For example, if you want to address the problem of affect control, the story is not about angry children or adults, but about an Indian tribe living in the Orinoco Delta, where they are repeatedly attacked by angry monkeys. The topic of "affect control" is developed in a story about monkeys.

One must choose a stage on which an enactment is possible and which is attractive. This could be a foreign culture, times past, alien people, ferocious animals, or an exotic region. Chances are that the audience is fascinated because the topos is not familiar. Suitable topos are those that promise drama and allow for different roles. Therefore, one must consider what could occur in a particular topos. In some topos, a lot can happen, and all kinds of drama can develop; other topos offer fewer possibilities.

For example, if we choose an oasis in the Sahara, the range of possible plots is small. Camels and dogs as animals might play a role, traders and smugglers might act as protagonists or key figures, palm trees might set the background, and a horrific sandstorm might approach. The oasis, however, might express extreme togetherness or the contrary, desperate loneliness.

The topos of a medieval city, on the other hand, has more to offer. It is easier to develop a story. With the Middle Ages, we associate mighty kings, wise queens, seductive princesses, courageous knights, vicious robbers, brutal raids, deadly famines, wild animals, tough fights, devasting diseases, magical castles, treacherous merchants, bawdy innkeepers, careless gamblers, shaggy beggars, voluptuous markets, etc. A vast number of associations come to our mind, and thus to the listeners, too. So, if we choose a stimulating topos, it is easier for the listeners to imagine the respective scenes and continue the story.

Deceptive truths

Children like to fantasise about animals. Africa is a suitable projection screen. Africa offers lions, giraffes, rhinos, apes, hippos, zebras, elephants, and buffaloes. Another topos with which we associate animals is Australia. There, crocodiles lurk in waters, koalas hide in trees, kangaroos leap across steppes, and emus forage for berries in eucalypt forests. The story can also be set in the deep, deep forest where foxes roam, deer run around, the bad, bad wolf crouches, and there is even a witch waiting to beguile passersby.

Young people prefer stories that are partially true. We then tell the story of the Briton Henry Worsley, who tried to cross Antarctica on cross-country skis and failed, or of the Japanese Lieutenant Onoda Hirō, who held out until 1974 on the Philippine island of Lubang after the end of the Second World War and did not realize that the war was over. We explain to the group that between 80 and 90 percent of the story is true, but we allowed ourselves to add between 10 and 20 percent fiction. Most of the time, at the end of the session, the young people want to know what was true and what we made up.

Protagonists and antagonists: hero, victim, mentor etc.

When we select or develop a story ourselves, we start off by giving the protagonists and antagonists a profile. They must be distinguishable in their behaviors and characteristics. We want them to leave an impression in the minds of the audience. This sounds obvious at first, but when one develops a story spontaneously, there is a tendency that the profiles of the characters converge, and differences become blurred. We ourselves do not notice this. On the contrary, we are convinced that we attribute distinctive features to the central characters. But because we have our preferences and are influenced by common clichés and ideologies, the profiles of the protagonists and antagonists tend to flatten out. It is interesting, for example, how today women characters in stories are predominantly portrayed as strong, combative, and autonomous. Over-obedient female characters hardly ever appear anymore, as this is currently considered politically incorrect.[9]

However, the aim in Mythodrama is to present diverse personalities, derived from different archetypical backgrounds. Since we do not usually possess the writerly greatness of William Shakespeare or Fyodor Dostoevsky, it is safer to rely on guidelines. One possibility is to consult archetypal patterns. We consult mythologies and sketch the characters accordingly. We might want to include a hero who is characterised by daring, oppositional tendency, overestimation, fear of being hurt, but is still determined to fulfill his noble motives. Conversely, the story can be about a victim. The victim is then the target of aggression, feels desperate, radiates self-pity, and sends out calls for help. The story can also feature a fatherly person who is serene, calm, seems supreme, wise, offers protection, but also harbors Zeusian claims to power and rage.

It is important that stories include mentors. These are figures who offer advice and support.

The basic rule is that the protagonists and antagonists one chooses or develops must be relevant to the group in question. The Mythodrama leader therefore sketches the characters based on the experiences of the children and young people. If the children or young people suffer because of colleagues who are aggressive, terrorize or bully everyone, then the

Mythodrama leader also picks a character that everyone in the story fears. He then introduces a character with a similar profile as experienced by the children or young people. This can be a hero or a villain. If secrets should be uncovered, the story might feature a witch who lives in the dark, dark forest and engages in forbidden activities.

In the stories we encounter in films, series, novellas, on the internet, in the tabloids and in politics, there are a wide spectrum of themes. Most of the time they are treated as dichotomies. They deal with opposites that are the cause of desperation, anger, frustration, but also excite us and get us going: good or evil, life or death, love or hate, truth or lies, arrival or departure, strength or weakness, loyalty or deceit, wisdom or stupidity and finally hope or despair. Most stories can be assigned to one of these opposites. This choice of themes reflects the existential challenges we face in life. They point to the fundamental issues of human beings: justice, conformity, power, aggression, rage, abuse, etc.

After the protagonists and antagonists have been introduced, the problem is defined. The stories usually start with a dilemma or a specific challenge. In most of the stories we use in Mythodrama, the protagonist is confronted with a difficulty for which he does not yet have an answer. He must find a magic stone in a valley but has no idea where or what the stone looks like; he is looking for his brother from whom he was separated when he was one year old and of whom he only knows that he is selling boxes, or he is trying to reconcile with someone but whom he personally dislikes but knows all his secrets. The problem presented at the beginning of the story calls for a solution, but one that is not easily found and does not spontaneously come to mind.

The choice of the appropriate story

The choice of story can be made in different ways. One possibility is to start from a well-known story. It can be an excerpt from literature, a play, a fairy tale, or a legend. In this case, however, the story does not have to be reproduced word by word and with the known story line but may be altered. Depending on the theme of the group, it can be extended, shortened, distorted, or only partially told. The known story thus merely serves as the basis for a story of one's own. As mentioned, the stories are used as a medium of contact or serve as a vessel for the topics and problems of the children and young people; we are not presenting educational stories or teaching literature. So, to steal and alter story lines is allowed! What is important is that the story concurs with the needs of the group and the Mythodrama leader.

The courage to create your own story

Mythodrama leaders are free to invent a story of their own if it meets the criteria laid out here. It helps to get inspired by real stories first. We might get our ideas from the news, a tabloid, or historical events. A hurricane in Florida might be an occasion to develop a story of a girl who lost her home because her parents were "blown away." Or, a news item of a 6-year-old girl who was charged with a huge fine because she was travelling on a public bus without a ticket and was not accompanied by an adult could be developed into a story about justice or injustice . The Mythodrama leader transforms such news items into a story that is presentable to the group.

Events in the distant past can also be a starting point for a story. The capture of the Aztec ruler Montezuma and the conquest of Tenochtitlan by Hernán Cortés is one way to introduce the theme of trust and betrayal; the fate of Marilyn Monroe or Kurt Cobain might be an occasion to dwell on unfulfilled love and the dangers being a celebrity. In this way, historical events and figures can serve as a template for a mythodramatic story.

With children, it is advisable to include details from their environment in the story. For example, if the story takes place in the past, one might mention an old house that exists in the children's world. It is also advisable to include well-known figures as antagonists; in Switzerland, this could be a train conductor, an alphorn player; in the U.S., this could be the baseball player Roger Clemens, the talk master Oprah Winfrey, or another celebrity the children or adolescents know.

The climax is the beginning of the imagination

Mythodramatic stories do not have an ending. The narrator stops relating the story just before the audience suspects that something uncanny or extraordinary is about to happen. They are curious to find out what will happen next. Instead of continuing the story, the narrator invites the participants to think for themselves how the story could continue. They are invited to imagine the continuation. They should concentrate on themselves and focus on the images that emerge before their inner eye. Mythodramatic stories thus stimulate imagination. The Mythodrama leader emphasizes, though, that there is no right or wrong in the story. Everything is possible, and the opposite is also allowed to occur: naughty, provocative, beautiful, embarrassing, banal, obscene, wonderful, amazing scenes. The children or young people are free to shape their sequel.

Narrative techniques

Being the center of everyone's attention with all eyes on you is not everyone's choice. Fears arise. What if I lose the thread, appear boring, my story doesn't convince the listeners, and I make a fool of myself? We don't always wish to be exposed and subjected to possible criticism.

To have reservations to recite a story by heart in front of a group is understandable. However, these hesitations are not only caused by a personal reluctance but also have to do with our communication habits. When we speak, we usually address a counterpart. We speak to a fellow human being whose facial expressions and gestures we keep an eye on and whose paraverbal expressions we register. If he or she responds with a nod or a smile, this supports our flow of speech. If he or she makes paraverbal statements such as "Aha," Mm," or So so," we are encouraged to continue. In this way, we protect ourselves from surprises such as being scolded, getting a look of disdain, or being laughed at. We don't take any risks when we communicate spontaneously and authentically. The way we speak is naturally influenced by the signals the listener sends. If they seem absent, this slows down our narrative flow, and we might fall silent. But if the other person signals interest and curiosity, then our tongue loosens.

We might even reveal more than we want to. Talking is an interactive process that we influence through our words and our behaviour.

When we tell a story to a group, these securities are lacking. One is alone. Because we can't align ourselves with several people at the same time, we expose ourselves. The speaker takes risks. We can lose the attention of the audience, bore, or annoy them. The speech is not generated by an interaction but turns into a one-man or one-woman show. For this reason, people who speak professionally in front of groups often prepare themselves meticulously. At seminars, presentations and in workshops, people use PowerPoints that determine the course of the speech and the content, and to which the audience is geared. Engaging with the audience becomes secondary. Detailed preparations help us deal with uncertainties, minimize imponderables, and enable us to abide to standards. One does nothing wrong and does not reveal personal weaknesses. At the same time, however, one hampers human encounters and might fail to connect emotionally with the audience.

When the storyteller becomes the story

It is not always easy to get a group of restless, often naughty children's or young people's attention. Not every child or adolescent is prepared to listen to a story. To take up the role of the storyteller is always a risk. Sometimes you fail and must handle frustrations. Frequently, the objection is made that physically present storytellers are outdated in the age of digitalization. Who wants to hear to the voice of an adult when there is an almost endless supply of films and entertainment? Children and young people hear and see enough stories, so an obvious conclusion could be that they can do without the attempts of a psychologist or social worker to tell them something exciting.

It is thus important to realize, that in Mythodrama the act of storytelling fulfills another function. We don't want to *entertain* children or young people but to facilitate interpersonal contacts. The stories serve as a way of tuning in to each other's moods and subjective feelings and start fantasizing. They deepen the relationship between the therapists and the children or young people and among group members. They are the bracket and the common denominator of the group. They are used as a psychological tool to evoke the so-called "imaginal groupale": the idea of being a collective psychological unit.[10]

To successfully tell a story to a group, the first and foremost factor is the *inner willingness* to take on the role of the storyteller. Children and young people cannot be told stories in passing or with a detached attitude. The storyteller must immerse himself or herself into the story and identify with it.

The storytelling act does not tolerate insecurities. It is therefore important to put aside ambivalences and personal concerns. Either one tells a story or one remains silent! It is important to try mobilizing a certain enthusiasm for the story. As a storyteller, you give yourself a "push," put aside your own sensitivities, and dedicate yourself 100 percent to the story. The narrator must appropriate the story mentally as well as emotionally. He or she represents the story with his or her whole personality.

The stories are neither read from a sheet of paper nor from a teleprompter but are memorized and then told spontaneously. The children and young people should have the impression that the story comes from the storyteller. In the perception of the children or young people, the group leader sits or stands in front of them, is completely focused on the group, and speaks freely while his or her gaze wanders from listener to listener. He or she becomes the living embodiment of the story.

As a reminder, the storyteller can put a DIN A5 sheet of paper with a mind-map on the floor in front of him or her. This paper should not contain sentences or detailed guidelines but only keywords and an overview of the structure of the story. If the speaker relies on more than one paper, there is a danger that he or she starts messing around with the sheets and distracting the attention of the listeners. The story no longer belongs to the storyteller but to the papers. Spontaneity suffers. However, if the story is told by heart, there is a good chance that the story will become a medium of contact. The narrator inevitably introduces his or her personality. He or she is then more likely to connect with the listeners on a deeper level. The group experiences him or her as a human being. This increases the chance of therapeutic effect.

The art of memory

There are several techniques that can be useful to ensure that storytelling is a success. As mentioned, memorizing the story is important. The trick is to connect the different scenes and characters with *personal experiences*, *scenes*, and *characters*. When preparing the story, one tries to find an acquaintance who roughly fits the profile of the protagonist and tries to recall a place, which is similar to the topos of the story. For example, if a part of the story takes place in a sordid flat, then you pick an apartment you experienced as disgusting. When you relate the particular story by heart, you then imagine the flat you personally know with your inner eye. Of course, you don't share this with the audience. However, placing the story in a familiar flat influences the quality of storytelling; the listeners notice that you are picturing a real flat in your mind's eye. The story becomes more personal, palpable, and convincing. You can follow the same procedure with the protagonists. It is easier to imagine a protagonist if you have a concrete person in mind. It should be someone you know but who is not too familiar to you. So don't choose your sister, wife or husband!

The advantage of these inner stand-ins is that it is a lot easier to describe the protagonist or place. If the narrative thread leads you to a flat, you imagine the flat you are acquainted with. When you see the flat or a person in your head, you don't have to think about the right words because you can describe the scene that you imagine. The story turns into a personal account, gains in spontaneity and accuracy.

Hearing, seeing, touching, tasting, and the sense of smell

When telling a story, we should refer to our five senses: hearing, seeing, touching, smelling and tasting. The corresponding organs provide us with information that constitutes our perceptions. Through the eyes, ears, nose, tongue, and skin, we receive signals that we interpret and shape. A sound does not remain an air vibration but becomes a gestalt that frightens, irritates, or delights us. We perceive ourselves and the world around us through our senses. To be alive means being able to immerse in these perceptions and draw conclusions. Thanks to our eyes, we see the green tips of the leaves of a palm tree; thanks to our bodily sensation, we feel the blowing of the wind, which rustles the palm leaves; thanks to our sense of smell, we register the smell of cake wafting through the house; and thanks to our tongue, we can enjoy the apple that lies before us. Our mind analyses the contents that are transferred to our brain by various sensory channels and gives them meaning.

Information that is delivered to us by a single organ carries less weight. If the garden hose on the lawn is not amplified by an acoustic signal, we pay less attention to it. We know how important hearing and seeing are for us. We are less aware of the influence of the smells we register unconsciously. Not only do decisions depend on the fragrances that prevail in a room, but odors also play a major role in the choice of a partner and the recollection of past experiences. If we can't smell someone, then we had better back off. Also, we are often unaware of the influence a gentle touch might have. Even a quick pat can change our mood and influence a decision. As a guest in a restaurant, we are more generous with the tip when the waiter touches us briefly, even if we do not notice.[11]

Stories become correspondingly more exciting when sensory perceptions are included. They give the listener an immediate impression of what is happening. Instead of saying, "He (the protagonist) falls into the house with the door and is frightened," it is advisable to say: "The door handle feels slippery. He nevertheless pushes it down using all his strength and rams the wooden door with his shoulder. There is a loud crash. He (the protagonist) loses his balance and falls headfirst into the house. He finds himself lying in the dark on the floor. He is unable to see but notices the greasy floor under his hands and takes a deep breath. Gradually, he manages to pick himself up, rubs his eyes and looks around. He detects a pale light on the wall. His jaw drops, his eyes are now wide open. He thinks: "This can't be happening!" Then suddenly, he detects a silhouette in the pale light . . ."

The art of storytelling is to point out sensory perceptions, which the listeners can interpret themselves. All four senses should be brought to the attention of the listeners. If in the story, someone climbs a tree, the storyteller mentions the rustling of the leaves, his gaze on a green meadow down below, perhaps refers to the fragrance of the roses, while he is breathing heavily. Stories should not be told dryly but be enriched with images, sounds, and smells.

Meanies, fools and heroes — who and how are they?

Stories thrive on heroes, cowards, robbers, cheats, creeps, bosses, machos, prima donnas, fools, magicians, helpers, and John Averages. In many stories the listeners are confronted with several archetypes. The group participants discover with whom they can identify or which figures resonate. In Mythodrama, children or young people then have the possibility to engage in depth with a preferred character. Children imagine they could be knights, adventurers, singers, a landlady, or a mother, or are fascinated and absorbed by a Mafia boss or a gangster. A character might become a role model or the contrary, a deterrent. Children or young people imagine what they would do or think if they were that person. To make it easier for them to identify with the characters of a story and become familiar with the setting, we sometimes invite children or young people to profile the characters in the story themselves before they hear the story. We present them caricatures of the figures that will appear in the story. They are then invited to give them features and describe their possible behaviour. They assign attributes to the protagonists and antagonists. They discuss and then decide which figures are cheeky, shy, rude, reckless, cautious, aggressive, harmless, boring, exciting, or well-behaved. They also choose the names of the figures. We deliberately created our stories in such a way that the personality profiles of the protagonists and antagonists are not clearly defined. The storyteller can then refer to the definitions and descriptions given by the group when telling the story. The children or young people are also invited to think about the origins of the characters. From their point of view, they then come from New York, ancient Athens, Zurich, Sigriswil, or Alice Springs. They often resort to stereotypes. They might call a character a bourgeois Swiss, a passionate Lebanese, a cheeky African, a stingy Scot, or a funny Indian. The group leader can also pause during the storytelling and invite the children or young people to think about what the character will now do or think. This approach facilitates identification with the characters in the story. The children or young people feel that it is their very own story they are hearing. They are the co-creators of the story!

Recognition facilitates phases of relaxation

Stories are characterised by a story line. The individual scenes are part of an overall plot. A good story is full of surprises and unusual actions. To understand the overall context, one has to keep to the story line. That means one must be attentive. The danger is that one might omit a detail of the story that is important. The story should have a certain suspense. At the same time, listeners also want to relax. The listeners cannot be permanently in suspense but need microbreaks. The narrator should therefore also insert moments and short scenes so the listeners can recline. One possibility is the repetition of phrases or distinct behavior. The storyteller uses the same wordings or movements when a certain figure appears. The listener then recognizes a sentence or an action and has the impression he or she is familiar with the figure. The narrator creates familiarity by repeating certain statements, gestures or behaviors of protagonists or antagonists. A protagonist might always exclaim, "This is dripple-dibel-dobel-dabel-dumm," when he or she makes a mistake or is afraid or responds to questions with the same answering line, "Boba doesn't know and Bubu doesn't bite. That means he's Gaga!" Especially younger children love such recurring allophonic elements. They trigger laughter and lead to a brief relaxation. Moods of the protagonists can be expressed by distinctive actions. For instance, the protagonist might express joy by demonstrating his "African bird dance."

Children like to be in motion. When they are among other children, this urge is intensified. To help them engage with the story, activities that occur in the story can be acted out briefly. For example, at the appropriate point, the Mythodrama leader suggests stomping and shouting across the room as the protagonist does in the story. Thanks to such short interventions, the children respond to their need for movement without losing contact with the story. They are active but still mentally connected to the story.

It is important that after the break is finished, the storyteller immediately communicates what happens next: "Now you close your eyes again listen. Let everyone thinks for themselves how the story will continue!" He or she gives such instructions in a calm but firm voice and reacts when a member of the group becomes restless by touching him briefly on the shoulders, arms, or back. When they are able to concentrate on the narrator again, they are usually calm.

Pauses and breaks help the listener to engage

The mythodramatic stories are rarely told without interruptions. The narrator can pause occasionally and invite the listeners to imagine what will happen next. How does the old woman react when she sees that a girl has smuggled herself onto the boat? What might be the meaning of the cracking noise the explorer overhears as he walks across the suspension bridge? The point is to involve the audience in the unfolding of the story. The storyteller might want to invite the children to reveal what their immediate reactions or thoughts.

However, it is better to allow only short pauses in order to keep the story line and suspense. The storyteller may also want to confront the listeners with a task. For example: The protagonist of the story is about to undertake a journey. She or he is allowed to carry three items with her or him that will fit into a small rucksack. The narrator then asks the children or young people to keep in mind what they would want to take with them. Such tasks give the listeners the opportunity to attribute something to the story themselves. Often the answers of children are very informative. It can be significant what a child or young person puts into a rucksack. A picture of the family? A cell phone? A pocketknife? A book? The audience expresses ideas, which might indicate what is important for them and what their resources are. The items chosen can be interpreted and linked to the personals lives of the participants in the processing phase of the Mythodrama.

Including references to the outside world

Since the Mythodrama leader narrates the story by heart, he or she can elaborate it and change it as he or she pleases. He or she can try to include details from the actual life of the children or young people without deviating from the story line. He or she might want to include a person that all the children are familiar with, describe a building the children are familiar with, or refer to an event that all of them have experienced. The narrator then states, for example, that the protagonist is standing in front of an entrance and notices that there is a statue of a demon grinning at him on the right side of the door. The narrator is aware that the entrance to the schoolhouse that the children attend is ornamented by such a demon. The children then recognize their own school.

If there is a trustful atmosphere in the group and the Mythodrama leader knows the participants well, names can be used for the antagonists that are similar to the names of the group participants. For example, if a boy in the group is called Bruno, then the narrator calls a figure Brunkivski. Of course, the narrator denies that this choice of name has anything to do with the Bruno in the group. The boy might be flattered because indirectly he is mentioned without being exposed or even be offended. Younger children in particular love to be included discreetly in a story.

Storytelling is bonding

As mentioned elsewhere, the story serves as a medium between the group leaders and the children. The stories don't need to abide to literature standards or be original. One of their purposes is to convey the moods, feelings, and complexes of the storyteller. The children or young people connect with the group leader via the story a lot more easily because the storyteller inadvertently reveals his psychological condition, idiosyncrasies, and personal proclivities. The children have a valuable opportunity to relate with an adult without having to care about educational issues, be bothered with age differences, having to adhere to goals, or abiding by rules. The chance is that this will lead to an authentic encounter between the adult and the child or young person.

The use of pictures

The narrator might want to use pictures to depict scenes, characters, or the location of the story. The topos of the story becomes tangible for the listeners when they have a picture in front of their eyes. For a story that takes place in Rio de Janeiro, we showed the young people pictures of the favelas in Rio. The children studied them and imagined what life in the favelas could be like and what the worries of the people living there are. In a story that took place in northern Canada, children were shown pictures of Baffin Island. They were able to study the bare mountains, snow, drifting icebergs and wonder how one survives in such an inhospitable environment. Images of the topos announce the mood for the story. If pictures are used as an interlude, care must be taken that the children's or young people's attention does not decrease and the flow of the story is interrupted.

The listeners should feel cleverer than the narrator

Storytellers dedicate themselves to the story. The goal is not to convince the listeners that one is a brilliant storyteller but to bring a story to life. The narrator must therefore be prepared to act fatuously or stupidly if the story demands it. The children or young people should have the impression that they are *superior* to the storyteller. They are less naive than he and detect dangers and challenges that he oversees: "Theo's was breathless: 'Wow! You still talk to me! So, you're not offended that I received the school prize and all money, that goes with it!' Theo had a tight grip on the box that lay in front of the door. 'A gift, a gift to me!' Theo wondered, though, why the box wasn't delivered to him personally. 'Probably he or she didn't have time and knew I was about to leave. Something was odd though, no letter was attached.' Theo held the box to his ear: He hears a strange ticking noise. As rips open the paper he detect wires and suddenly realizes …"

Of course, the story implies that Theo was sent a bomb. However, the storyteller should pretend not to realise this. Passages that allow the audience to feel smarter than the narrator create attention and suspense. The storyteller pretends not to grasp the warning signals or hints that suggest danger or unpleasant events are approaching. The listeners then are intrigued and mobilize their own detective instincts.

Employ primary and secondary scenarios

It is useful when a story consists of two corresponding story lines: the main story line and a sidetrack that might turn out to be equally important. The main stage and the sideshow might at first by completely separate. As the story evolves, the two stories might converge, though.

Technically, the narrator can begin by starting with one story line. At a certain point, generally when something is about to happen, he or she stops and continues with the second story or an alternative version in order to return to the main story line later on. For example, he or she starts with a story about a woodsman in Canada who believes that you can talk to the wolves and bears if you have the right attitude and are friendly to them.

"He's stalking through a snow-covered landscape in the Yukon and he repeats to himself, "If I get attacked by a bear, all I have to do is use my special talent." He stares into the distance, spots mountains while trudging through the snow, clinging to his GPS and checking to see if he is connected. He detects traces in the snow. Are these paws or footsteps? He is curious. He bows when he hears a stomping sound behind him. "What could this be?" He turns around. . . . Meanwhile, nearby in a log cabin a boy warbles a song to himself as he gambols. He looks out the window and thinks: 'Does this winter never end? Why did my parents move to the Yukon?' He devotes himself to a computer game that was developed in Siberia. He is very good at it. Today, however, the screen flickers. Something is odd. He makes a restart, but the screen still flickers and then, all of a sudden, he hears a desperate voice from his computer . . ."

At this point the narrator might return to the main thread, and the story continues. In this story, the boy is finally able to help the forester because he has a melody that calms bears in his Siberian computer game. However, telling a story with two story lines is only successful when one of the stories remains the key story. The second story should be a substory.

Expressing feelings and mood through details

"You are sitting in an airplane and flying over the Amazon at a low altitude. 'How much longer is this going to take?' exclaims Getrud Hegetschwiler from Bad Kreuznach, casting a glance out of the window. 'Forest, forest, forest — how boring. There's not even wine here, like at home. Didn't the tour guide promise that we would see a mountain with an amazing waterfall?' Getrud stares down at the endless forest. But what is that? Getrud presses her nose against the window and peers down. 'Surely that doesn't exist! She gasps, and her heart pounds. No, that is not possible. She looks around. The other passengers remain quiet. She gazes out of the window once more and at the forest more closely. What is happening? The plane seems to lose altitude. . . Two weeks later, she is sitting at a shaky table in Porto Allegro. She is content. Pedro sits next to her. She holds his hand. Obviously, she is attached to him and grateful for what he has done for her."

Stories create suspense when the main events are not related but merely hinted at. The story line progresses towards an event only to stop short of it. The audience can then imagine what might have happened.

Further, it is important in this context that moods and feelings are not explicitly expressed but by describing the particular gestures and facial expressions of the person concerned. Instead of saying "She is afraid," she starts to sweat, trembles, and has her eyes wide open. The words "She is afraid" should not be employed; it is more advisable to place hints.

The use of mental movers

Another characteristic of mythodramatic stories are the *mental movers*. These are small additions that do not seem to comply with the story line — an element that one cannot understand based on the story, that does not make sense. For example: The protagonist is walking along a narrow country lane. She wants to buy a loaf of bread at the nearby grocery shop. When she reaches the shop, a man dressed in red stands in front of the door, raises his voice and says: "I'm a VCR, too! Don't forget that!" The woman shakes her head and hurries past him.

The purpose of such bizarre details is to trigger cognitive dissonance in the listeners. They ponder whether there is a connection between this and the story line. Often, they trigger perplexity. Children and young people begin to brood and look for connections. The explanations they develop often reveal something about their personality and mental resources. They indicate how the child or young person thinks and what solutions to his or her problem might be possible. However, it often happens that such slight craziness is overheard: We tend to hear what we already know and understand.

ENDNOTES

[1] C. von Schaik & K. Michel, *The Good Book about Human Nature.*

[2] K. Oatley, *Such Stuff as Dreams. The Psychology of Fiction.*

[3] D. Gelernter, *The Tides of Mind. Uncovering the Spectrum of Consciousness.*

[4] A. Stevens, "The Archetypes" Ed. Papadopoulos, Renos, *The Handbook of Jungian Psychology*, Chapter 3.

[5] Native American people whose historic territory includes parts of Wisconsin, Minnesota and Illinois. P. Radin, *The Winnebago Tribe.*

[6] G. Paris, *Wisdom of Psyche.* p. 29.

[7] C.R. Sunstein, *Why Societies Need Dissent.*

[8] J. Haidt, *The Happiness Hypothesis*, p. 69.

[9] D. Murray, *The Madness of Crowds. Gender, Race and Identity.*

[10] D. Anzieu, *The Group and the Unconscious.*

[11] M. Lim & K. Mynier, "Effect of server posture on restaurant tipping," *Journal of Applied Social Psychology*, Vol. 23, Issue 8 April 1993, pp. 678–685.

5

Phase Four: Being Carried Away by Fantasies — the Imagination

Summary

In this chapter, the fourth phase of Mythodrama is explained and described. The way children or young people are encouraged to imagine. Imagination is understood as the ability to generate new ideas and develop images that help us to understand ourselves, our inner worlds. Imagination is placed in an overall social context, and its significance for group psychotherapy is examined.

What distinguishes humans from animals? It is well known that we share 99 percent of our genetic material with our closest relatives, the chimpanzees. Darwin's disciple, Huxley[1] was convinced two centuries ago that our actions, decisions, and emotions are biologically determined and that the notion of self-control is an illusion. According to Darwin's theory of evolution[2], genetic mutations steer human development and not the mind, which was considered a residue of our brain activities.

Our self-perception differs from Huxley's view. According to our perception, the differences from primates are gigantic: We humans make decisions, walk upright, dress ourselves, live in insulated houses, move around in metal enclosures in which we burn the remains of dinosaurs, crowd ourselves into round constructions that carry us through the air, and spend endless time exchanging sounds and signs. We experience ourselves as distinct, even though we realise that we share a lot with the animal world. Even during Darwin's time, in contrast to Huxley, some of his students emphasised differences and considered the mind as crucial to human development. Darwin's student, Wallace[3] believed that the mind was of paramount importance. The intellect was considered the initiator of development and unique among all living beings. In more recent times, this particular view has been confirmed by ethology. Our closest relatives are incapable of reflecting about themselves. Most importantly, we can undertake *mental trips*. In our mind, we can leave a current situation, explore future scenarios, or return to the past. We are not just caught up in the present, but mentally we can cross time boundaries, transfer ourselves into unknown places, groups, and even pretend being someone else! This mental flexibility is unique. These mental trips consist, of course, of inner images. We immerse ourselves in the inner, subjective world. We might imagine something new or revive a memory. What is apparently extraordinary is that the imagined scenes often have the character of a *vocation*. The images release inner dynamics, which motivate us to set new goals. We want to fulfill what we have developed in our minds. Fantasies are thus the root cause of our actions and plans.[4] The ability to mentally beam ourselves to distant places and picture ourselves in other sceneries gives us drive but also makes us a slightly crazy. We don't comply with the situations we are in entirely but might want to act out a fantasy. Our actions and motives are thus not only derived from the reality of life but are also based on imagination. Thanks to them, we reshape our lives, leave dwellings, destroy our surroundings, experiment with materials, climb mountains and start projects. It is not sober reality that drives us but imaginations that transcend our very existence.

In the fourth phase of Mythodrama, this ability is used creatively. The stories help children and adolescents to drift away and turn their focus inwards. While they are listening to the story, they might be gradually carried away into another world. The storyteller then stops at a certain point and invites the listeners to imagine its continuation. The group is asked to envision how the story will end. What they have imagined will be spun out further. Here are some examples of children's and young people's imaginations during the fourth phase of a Mythodrama group session:

Boy, 10 years: "The house on the island is lopsided, it has a strange red roof. Edmund goes to the strange house and knocks on a door. A man steps out. Edmund withdraws, his jaw drops. The man looks scary, especially his face. Where did he get that scrape? Edmund clutches his laser pistol! He is trembling. 'Shall I?' Now there is a loud bang and roaring laughter . . ."

Boy, 8 years old: "There's shit everywhere, there's shit on everyone, there's shit on the lamps, on the trees, on the houses, on the cars. Barnie comes and destroys everything; finally there's nothing left, just shit, shit. Barnie is all alone. Suddenly, there is a gust of wind and a jet, Barnie is lifted into the air, spun in a circle and is suddenly in a spaceship. There's a wedding couple standing next to him. They're giggling . . .'

Girl, 13: "There are big fish in this part of the sea. Some of them are aggressive. Especially when you have bad thoughts, they attack you. The knocking is coming from one such fish. I am standing on the bow of the ship, the front part of the ship is damaged because of a collision, water is seeping through the cracks in the hull of the ship. Finally, I jump into the water and wave to my colleague, who jumps after me. We are both in the water swimming and see an island in front of us."

The above imaginings are continuations of different stories The Mythodrama leader stopped at a point where an event is hinted at. These cliffhangers sometimes cause a slight tension among children or young people. They might want the storyteller to tell them how the story goes on. The Mythodrama leader can promise this to them but should insist that they should first develop their endings. Anything is possible, even the opposite, he might add. He explains to the children that they should listen to themselves and follow the images that the story triggered in them.

To be able to fantasize, the children or young people have to feel comfortable. Depending on the room, this is done in different ways. If the session is held in a room with carpets and cushions, the children or young people can lie down on the floor or stretch out on mattresses provided. Children like to crawl behind cushions or throw them at each other. If the story is being told in a classroom or conference hall, then the imagination phase should begin with precise instructions, what position the children or young people should choose. If they are sitting behind school desks, then the Mythodrama leader asks them to place their heads in their folded forearms on the desk before closing their eyes. This instruction should be given in a firm voice, as chaos must be prevented. In this way, the children or young people are more likely to carry out what is expected of them. Adolescents and adults are willing to comply with this request. Younger children and school classes, on the other hand, tend to get distracted by what else is happening in the room. To prevent this, it is advisable to place the children at a safe distance from each other.

The tone of the Mythodrama leader's voice determines whether children or young people can join in, relax, and fantasize. Preferably he gives his instructions in a calm voice, including bodily feelings and sensations: "Your right arm is now very heavy;" "You are breathing deeply in and out"; "You have the feeling of sinking into the ground"; "You are completely relaxed"; "You stretch your limbs as far as you can." The more relaxed the listeners are, the greater the chance that inner images will emerge and can be observed. They cannot be the result of a deliberate act but should emerge spontaneously. Soul should be the creator of the inner drama.

Children imagine in a different way from adults and adolescents. Imagination, understood as a state in which one is absorbed by inner images and ignores the outside world, is perceived by some of them as unnatural. Since they possess less ego control, they are not always capable of distancing themselves from their surroundings. However, when they concentrate on the story, they imagine without realising it. In their awareness, they are still dealing with an external issue, the story. The story therefore acts as a catalyst. The children resort to unconscious images without being aware of it. They are actually engaging in active imagination.

Example

In his ending, a boy locked the protagonist in the cellar of a school building. In his imagination, the school building subsequently collapsed on the boy. His scene expressed his current situation quite precisely. He had great difficulties at school, which were augmented by family problems. His personal feelings corresponded to those of the protagonist: in the basement. However, in the end of his story, the protagonist has a secret weapon: He could transform himself into another person. This was an important indication for us that he still had his own powers to master his problems.

Cheating as a group experience

Children often cannot name the source of their products. Did they fantasize the scene themselves? Did they copy the picture of a colleague? They might copy each other. Often it is difficult for the Mythodrama leader to distinguish whether a version of the ending originates in the child in question. In the story of the boat trip, three children presented an identical ending: The ship got attacked by pirates, and all passengers were thrown overboard to the sharks! Coincidence? When working with children or young people, this question is of minor importance. Everything that the participants derive from the story is potentially meaningful. If children copy each other's end of the story, this might reveal something about their mood or state of mind. The children are tuned in to a group issue. In the ending with the sharks, the children wanted to experience themselves as a group. The wanted their distinct profile. One can only decide about the personal relevance of a conclusion after a dialogue with the child concerned. The prerequisite is a personal contact and knowledge of the social background of the child in question.

Provocative, harmless, extreme, or banal: Every conclusion is permitted

The willingness to pursue inner images is greater in adolescents than in children. However, the setting and the mood that prevails in the group has a big influence. Imagining is easier in a pleasant, humorous, and relaxed atmosphere. The Mythodrama leader should therefore not convey a deadly serious mood but take it — in the language of the young people—"easy." It can happen, however, that the children or young people are gripped by the ambition to develop an extraordinary ending. They want to make a name for themselves among their peers. They strain to present the most original ending possible or want to find out which ending is correct. The leader of the Mythodrama will counteract in such cases. He emphasizes that there are no correct or false conclusions. Also, gender differences are the norm: Girls tend to fantasize relationship dramas. Their endings deal, according to my experience, more with human conflicts: friendships that break up, bullying that is not being detected, bad-mouthing, and betrayals. Boys are attracted by extreme events. They imagine daring adventures, catastrophic explosions, and ruthless fights.[5] In contrast to the girls, they often want to impress with their conclusions. They want to provoke and therefore fantasise violence and sexual scenes. The reasons for these gender differences are highly debated. It is important therefore not to value these observations or become biased.

Rooms: The art of slight disorder

In Mythodrama, the size, design, and level of tidiness of the room in which the session is held play a role. Rooms in which participants can easily move around are suitable. In schools, these are often the sports or singing halls. Rooms with a large open space allow the children or adolescents to move around. What is kept in the room might influence the mood. In general, we prefer blank rooms, with no pictures on the wall and hardly any furniture. What helps children and adolescents to feel relaxed are items that indicate that they can take it easy. A number of cushions is ideal. They signal that regression, even fooling around, to make jokes, and play are options. During my work as head of the group psychotherapy department at the Cantonal Educational Counseling Center in Bern, we had the fortune to have large basement rooms. They were accessible via a narrow staircase, which led to subterranean floor. The children enjoyed the climbing down the stairs, which felt like entering the underworld. Each of the five subterranean rooms had a different floor plan and served a different function, which helped to organize the activities. Conversations took place in the disco room, the story endings were performed on the small stage in the anteroom, the room in which the story was completely blank but offered many pillows, and one room was reserved to dress up. However, Mythodrama can also be done in small rooms or even one's own consultation room or in a classroom. What matters is what the walls, furniture, and other objects radiate. A room that is *too* clinical or *too* tidy, though, might inhibit imagination. Children then start to adapt. A slight disorder and objects that serve no immediate purpose, though, might stimulate imagination. Perhaps there is an African wooden statue on a bookcase, a picture of a torero hanging on the wall, or a box of chocolates on the desk. The reason is that facilities send messages. A meticulously clean and tidy room might intimidate the participants. They feel nothing is allowed and the Mythodrama leader has everything under control while they are struggling with life.

When the children or young people are still tense, it's harder for them to imagine and continue the story. In such situations the group leader might want to add riddles or tasks. Just after having finished the story, he might point out that certain objects or phrases could appear in their story. For example, he mentions that the phrase "There are still fresh tomatoes in the grocery store" or "Are you sure the bridge will hold?" or "However, I would do anything if I were you!" could occur in the story. When participants fantasize about the story's continuation, they might incorporate such sentences. The Mythodrama leader can also suggest objects or people that can be integrated into their conclusions: a yellow old car, two nagging old women, or a policeman dressed in a ballet costume. The more absurd, the more likely it is that the children will be encouraged to accept the suggestions and then develop something of their own.

Practice has shown that school classes sometimes expect such hints. The danger is, though, that they will perceive the exercise as a lesson or that they will interfere with each other. If they must integrate concrete sentences into their conclusions, the hope is that they will rely on the fantasy to find a solution.

The constructive and destructive power of imagination

In Mythodrama, stories are used to activate imagination. Like going to the movies or watching Netflix, they transfer us into another world. This turn to our inner world connects us with our inner resources. When focusing on what emerges in front of our inner eye, we enrich the scenarios of the story we hear.

For instance, the storyteller might recount a story about a mountainous village. In our mind, perhaps, memories of a village that we visited during a vacation some years ago appears. We see a village like Juf or Disentis in front of our inner eye or recall a settlement in the mountains of Georgia. The theme of the story triggers memories. These are augmented, enriched, distorted, or amplified by our fantasies. What seems like a memory might be an imagined scene. By our own account, we are somewhere else, although physically we did not move. This ability to deepen or escape reality helps us to overcome troubles and strifes, confront dangers, set new goals, and give our lives meaning. Imagination is the key to overcoming personal difficulties. Therefore, before explaining the next stage of Mythodrama, we elaborate in depth the psychological significance of imagination.

To show the influence of imagination on our thoughts and actions, we start with a sad story. The tragic fate of the *Antarctic explorer Henry Worsley (1960-2016)*. His obsession and his uncompromising dedication to an idea exemplify the influence imagination can have on us. Worsley exemplifies the positive and negative effects of imagination.

"Always a little further . . ., a little further" was a phrase Worsley repeated in his head while pushing one ski in front of the other. The phrase served him like a mantra. He was in great pain, suffered under the unbearable cold and icy winds. The phrase helped him block out the monotonous snowy landscape around him. In front of him, beside and behind him stretched an endless expanse of snow, snow, and more snow. An icy wind blew in his face and, since he had lost a tooth, directly into his mouth. The cold was unbearable. Weakened by the effort and sick, he advanced only slowly. Despite the hellish agony, however, he refused to press the emergency button and call for help. Nothing dissuaded Henry Worsley, the British ex-soldier, from his plan. He was going to cross Antarctica single-handedly! He had prepared himself well. He had trained on Baffin Island in Canada and had also made inquiries about all the dangers. Nothing should go wrong. After 71 days of physical exertion, Worsley collapsed just before the finish line. Not only was he dehydrated and debilitated, but he was also suffering from bacterial peritonitis. Worsley died a few days after his evacuation in Punta Arenas, Chile. He was unable to fulfill his dream.

A cross-country trip on skis across the South Pole is not everyone's cup of tea. Readers will probably agree with me that Worsley's undertaking was slightly insane. No one asked him to cross Antarctica on cross-country skis. For most of us, it is inconceivable to voluntarily endure such cruel hardships. Moreover, the personal benefit of crossing Antarctica is practically zero. Why is anyone so crazy to start such an undertaking. Where does he get the strength to start such an enterprise, to leave his family life behind him, and risk his life at the other end of the world? Antarctica was not on the agenda during his upbringing, nor a topic in his social environment.

Our quite normal follies

Worsley is an example of extreme willpower and determination. Interesting for us is what made him to decide to travel to Antarctica. It was not money, neither fame nor other personal benefits; his strength of mind was based on a *fantasy*. Such examples are a manifestation of the power of imagination. Our actions and goals derive often from scenes we entertain in our heads. We reach extraordinary goals, cope with un-believable challenges and survive in extreme condition with the help of imagination. We not only adapt to harsh conditions and optimize our life situation, but we are also quite prone to slightly crazy actions. We are able to be selfless, but also self-destructive, because of imagination. We reach for goals beyond our social settings and comfort zones. Our decisions do not always serve our well-being or interests but are an expression of imagination. We dare things that endanger our health, complicate our everyday lives and are not comprehensible to outsiders. In other words, due to imagination, we are "not quite normal."

The actions we undertake and goals we set can be irrational, and many are harmless. The English eccentric John Slater decided to walk in striped pajamas from the southwestern most to the northwesternmost tip of Great Britain, from Lands End to John O'Groats. Other behaviors make us shake our heads in disbelief: climbing skyscrapers without securing, entering a car race between Bern and Zurich, and the like. All these are actions derive from imagined scenes.

Imagination also leads to changes in our personal lives. The chief physician of a hospital in Bern always dreamt of becoming a truck driver, roaming the autobahns, and crossing Europe. He finally quit his well-paid job in a clinic and sat behind the steering wheel of a big truck for a couple of years. A teacher in a rural town in Zürich dreamt of a life with the Pueblos of New Mexico, he gave up his job, crossed the Atlantic, and joined an Indian tribe. Paul Gauguin (1848-1904) left his family and left for French Polynesia to paint natives. He dreamt of a life in the wilderness surrounded by beautiful women. We humans long for extraordinary experiences or challenges, even when our lives are comfortable. Something in us makes us choose extraordinary paths and abide to programmed societal guidelines.

The search for the extraordinary, however, does not usually lead to radical changes in our lives or engage in daring projects. Generally, we are more careful and conscientious. But even if we don't turn our lives upside down, that doesn't mean that the need for the unfamiliar doesn't lurk in the depths of our soul. The desire to dive into another world can be lived discreetly. One follows a dream without causing ruptures or a scandal. Our desire to experience something special can be satisfied by booking an exotic trip. We fly to Belize to experience tropical swamps, master a part of the pilgrimage way to Santiago de Compostela, or set out for a mountain bike tour in the Livigno valley in Italy. The extraordinary is lived within the framework of order.

Why is breaking out of the daily grind attractive? Why don't we remain in our comfort zone? We trace our behaviour back to motives. We identify them as the guiding and driving psychological reasons.[6] We are driven by a variety of motives. They differ in quality, effect, and profile. In psychology, we speak of drives, desires, hormonal effects, and will. Whether we do something of our own accord or due to external reasons is often not clear. This is because most of our actions are not entirely the result of an inner urge. We fulfill internalized social expectations, obey rules, and fulfill duties. Most often, there is more than one motive behind a decision. We buy a bottle of wine in a store because the offer convinces us and, of course, because a drop of red wine belongs with a good meal. We buy an alarm system because there has an epidemic of been break-ins in the neighborhood but also because we might be a bit paranoid.

Phase Four: Being Carried Away by Fantasies — the Imagination

Some actions are caused by an inner impulse; others are a result of external pressure. Students take to their homework because there is a threat of unpleasant consequences, drivers slow down because they fear fines. We all adapt to the rules and expectations of the group to which we belong. We submit because we want to remain part of a community, do not want to be ostracized.

But what makes us engage in something completely different? Say or do something that is not common in our group of people? This is harder to find out because we tend to avoid straight answers when it comes to unusual and socially not accepted behaviour. We make up an explanation to legitimise the actions. Therefore, the declared reasons often are not sufficient to bring light into our motives. "Because it's there!" declared the famous British mountaineer George Mallory (1886-1924) when asked why he was climbing Mount Everest. He was perhaps aware that even a more complicated explanation would not reflect his motives. What we say about why we do something is often not the true reason for our action. We use language not only to explain ourselves but also to disguise our deeper reasons. A well-known rower convincingly explained that she was crossing the Atlantic in a rowboat to draw attention to ocean pollution. This sounded good to the ears of the public. However, actually she mainly wanted to be noticed, gain fame, and escape the drudgery at home. We like to disguise private, selfish, or amoral motives with the help of noble justifications.[7] There is a danger that we deceive ourselves. This happens to us every day with minor issues. We are convinced that we are on a diet but then devour a delicious Black Forest cake when neighbors appear: It would be a real shame to refuse the most generous offer by these friendly neighbors!

When we notice such discrepancies in ourselves, we look for external reasons and try to find excuses. We want to maintain our self-image. According to this thinking, we the commander of our actions. We understand what we do as the result of conscious decisions. However, from a psychological point of view, this is often not the case. Just as our self-image is not an objective reflection of our personality, our declared intentions often do not correspond to our real motives.

One reason is that we are not controlled by an all-powerful command center in our brain but by various forces. There are motives we accept, others of which we are ashamed, or even despise. Sigmund Freud therefore developed a model of psyche. He distinguished the id, ego, and superego, which contest each other for influence. Abraham Maslow established a hierarchy of needs, which represents the priority of desires, and C. G. Jung identified complexes that influence our behavior. In our professional as well as in our private lives, we therefore carry out orders of different authorities. We ourselves often do not recognize which motive has prevailed. We might feel an impulse and then be compelled to a certain action. Often, or maybe most of the time, we don't question our urge because at the same time, we were supplied with a reasonable explanation. Often it is hard to distinguish whether the explanation was fabricated or whether it expresses the truth.

Usually one differentiates between extrinsic and intrinsic motives. Extrinsic is defined as external incentives that trigger an action. We fear consequences, hope for material gain, or prestige. What we do is a result of our social context. An action is performed without innate involvement. In contrast, intrinsic motivations cannot be traced to external causes. They develop from within. Intrinsic motives include hunger, thirst, sexual desires, and perhaps the need to assert ourselves. However, most actions are triggered by a combination of extrinsic and intrinsic motives. The more motives conflate, the more likely we get active. The motives may coincide or contradict each other. We buy an electric car to demonstrate our environmental awareness, and at the same time we fulfill our desire for personal freedom and want to impress a brother-in-law.

The longing for borderline experiences

Back to Worsley: His motivation to start his horrendous trip is interesting. His fascination for Antarctica was aroused by the records of Ernest Shackleton (1874-1922). As a youth, he read the notes of this Antarctic explorer and was deeply impressed[8] Not only did he admire the coura-geous rescue of the men on Elephant Island but also Shackleton's leadership and willpower. From Worsley's point of view, Shackleton accomplished great deeds, even though he failed miserably in his actual endeavour. He did not cross Antarctica, but he managed to lead his crew so they survived the winter in the dark Antarctic unscathed before crossing over to Elephant Island in their wooden boats in a breakneck journey. Shackleton then ventured in a lifeboat on an adventurous crossing to South Georgia to get help for his shipwrecked men. Even in his lifetime, Shackleton was considered a hero and received a triumphant reception in both Buenos Aires and London. Henry Worsley was mesmerized by Shackleton's reports. He imagined the endless ice deserts of Antarctica that surrounded Shackleton's men, their struggle against snow and ice, the terrible hardships they endured, and the ingenuity with which Shackleton led the men. Henry Worsley based his personal mission on the fantasies he had while reading Shackleton's report. He concluded that he was the one who would complete Shackleton's project!

Worsley is an example of our principal source of motivation: imagination. Our ability to develop inner images stimulate us and give us orientation. Verena Kast[9] terms this capability the "inner space of freedom." We develop scenes into which we can subsequently mentally transfer ourselves. In many cases, these are sequences of images that have no connection with our lives. In our heads, we travel to strange and un-known worlds and undertake wonderful journeys. We create scenes spontaneously under guidance or semiconsciously. They are only accessible to us. In 1794, in his Wissenschaftslehre, Johann Gottlieb Fichte[10] describes imagination as the "possibility of our consciousness, our life, our being for ourselves."[11]

Imagination is described as a force thanks to which children master challenging situations at an early age. They imagine themselves into the future and imagine possible ways of reacting[12] Singer emphasizes the importance of imagination in therapies to gain access to unconscious material. Imagination helps to get in contact with patients and their body awareness.[13] Often the contents of imagination contain energy. They then influence our decisions and might even become the goal of our actions. They have a prompting character. Reality is expected to adapt to imagination. We thus leave the mode of adaptation and in many cases strive for goals outside our habits and social role.

For Worsley, Shackleton's narratives triggered fantasies. He put himself in his place and adopted his purpose. The images that rose in Worsley's mind as he read Shackleton's accounts were overwhelming to him and initiated his personal project. He left his comfort zone and sought out the inhospitable Antarctic, which became a projection screen for a personal challenge. He gave himself the task of completing Shackleton's project. An imagination had him it its grip.

The power of the imagination is evident not only in men and women who venture on adventurous journeys but in all aspects of life. Generally, the consequences are less dramatic. Worsley's example is therefore extreme but can serve as a metaphor to show the effects of potent fantasies. The basis of our behaviour lies often in the scenes we imagine in our heads.

Therefore, it is important to include intrapsychic processes in therapy. Children and adolescents can be helped in their problems, provided we take care of what is going on inside them. Imagination is an important resource, the "basic material for self-efficacy expectations."[14] Imaginations can initiate changes in attitude and healing processes.[15] When patients start to imagine, there is hope for healing. Being able to imagine that something could be different is the first step toward improving one's life situation.

Imagination is applied in different ways in therapy. In active imagination, the patient is asked to imagine spontaneously on a topic. The starting point can be an issue or a body sensation. Leuner[16] chose a different approach. He suggests metaphors and distinct scenes that encourage patients to imagine. He told me years ago that the choice of the appropriate initial image is crucial for catathymic imagery.

The power of imagination makes us unique

The ability to imagine distinguishes us from the animal world. Animals don't possess a comparable mental power, according to today's scientific knowledge.[17] It seems we are the sole beings on Earth that orient themselves not only to external realities but also to imagined scenes. We base decisions on scenes that have no connection to reality. These scenes influence our thinking and behaviour. As a result, we dare undertakings and make conclusions based on fantasies. Imaginations turn us into dreamers who want to change the world, researchers who realize innovations, entrepreneurs who create new products, grumblers who are convinced that everything could be better, doom mongers who expect the worst, or rebels who are determined to overthrow the prevailing order. Our ability to imagine is both a curse and a blessing.

Imagination journeys are anarchistic

Fantasies can be naughty, bizarre, strange, wonderful, expectational, surprising, boring, or crazy. Everything is possible, also the opposite. Often, they impose themselves on us without warning, exhilarate, frighten, or astonish us. Imaginations are not curbed by the norms and codes that characterise societies. However, it depends on our attitude whether we become aware of them and how we deal with them. We can ignore them, fight them, study them, or value them as a resource. Many imaginations contain ideas that enrich our lives. They help us set different priorities and alter perspectives. They may initiate radical changes of direction or trivial actions that give life a different quality. Some time ago, I observed a scene in a sparsely patronized suburban café that revealed the power of imagination:

Two champagne glasses were on the table. The elderly couple nodded to each other as they raised their glasses. They toasted each other and smiled. Their looks expressed a sublime contentment. The couple didn't seem to care about the world around them; this moment was precious to them. Did they have something to celebrate? It was all about them as a couple. The café was located between two huge, soulless apartment towers right next to a parking lot and a garage. It was hard to imagine a bleaker environment. The couple, however, radiated a sense of happiness. They were experiencing a climax as a couple that brightened their everyday lives and blessed them with this special moment. The couple's contentment contrasted sharply with the monotony and sadness of their surroundings. The pause, the drinking of the champagne was possible because of the fantasy the couple shared. They imagined themselves in another world; perhaps they felt like members of the haute society, staged the grandeur of life. The couple shared discreetly a mutual fantasy. Their imagination enriched their lives.

For us to perform or consider a fantasy, several motives must be addressed. One inner image is not enough to take the scepter. Worsley was obsessed by the idea of crossing Antarctica, but he pursued his plan also because of other motives. In his last communication to his wife, Worsley pictured himself embarking on lecture tours. Perhaps he imagined himself walking proudly down Fulham High Street in London and being considered a celebrity. We execute an idea when it is supported by various motives Usually a single motive cannot convince us to start hell tours.

The enchantment of our existence

How we deal with imaginations, however, varies and depends on personality, circumstances, social settings, and personal acceptance. Spontaneous imaginations are interpreted, reframed, and prioritized according to the perceptions, which serve as pattern to understanding the world. When an imagination overwhelms us, experiences get a different coloring. A skiing trip to the Matterhorn is no more just a physical workout but an enthralling experience, a chance to devour the majestic qualities of the Alps. The Alps radiate a special energy because of our ability to imagine. We feel we are connected with something greater, sense the sublime, and might even be emotionally touched when we gaze at the wonderful snow-covered peaks standing on a platform of a cable car station. Thanks to imagination, even dead peaks become animated!

Often, we do not realize that imagination is influencing us. It has an impact on our perceptions and judgments without us realizing it. Suppose we want to spend a weekend in Ticino. We study a hotel at the Scala of Ascona and look at the pictures of the hotel rooms and the reception. The photos include couples happily promenading in front of the lake. We might be convinced that our choice of hotel is based on facts; the price, the design, the location, and promised services. However, there is a chance that unconsciously we are influenced by inner images; they influence our perception and might even have no connection with what we see and facts. The hotel might remind us of a romantic scene in a movie, or the boardwalk recalls an experience of a friend who was robbed on the street in Barcelona. Both the movie and the friend's story influence our judgment. Perhaps pleasant memories of the movie compete with the friend's account. The images and information of the hotel in Ascona evoked hidden fantasies. Personally, we might still be absolutely convinced our judgment is based on facts and rational arguments, when actually we were confronted with and manipulated by inner discernments. The conclusions then are not the result of a sober analysis but rather of spontaneous images and scenes.

Eccentric interests and hobbies

Inner images also influence the way we spend our leisure time, follow interests, and pursue hobbies. For this reason, many activities we engage in are incomprehensible to outsiders. We invest time, energy, and money in a subject that causes our peers to scratch their heads and react puzzledly. One woman I met spent her life collecting figurines of elephants: large, small, artistic, cuddly, realistic. Finally, her basement and attic were full of small elephant figurines. She had packed them all in boxes and hoped that other people might be interested in them. She wanted to donate them to a museum. The problem: Nobody was interested. She wanted to give the figurines away, but there was zero interest in them! The collection was a result of her elephant fantasy. Another man studied the history and fauna of remote islands every night. He couldn't learn enough about the islands of Marion, Bounty, Clipperton, or others. He spent hours reading internet reports and studying photos of explorers who had discovered remote islands. His tragedy: He couldn't share his knowledge with anyone because nobody was interested in the migrations of seals on the Kerguelen Islands in such detail or the geology of Deception Island. Collecting elephant figurines or interest in remote islands carries little prestige and is hardly advantageous to a career, as is the case with other offbeat hobbies such as swamp soccer, eating nettles, spitting contests, extreme ironing, or collecting vomit bags. People choose subjects outside the interest spectrum of their environment because they are stimulated by a fantasy. Their interest is based on an inner image.

Internal ideas influence decisions

When we must choose among several possibilities, we develop ideas about what the consequences of a choice might be. We therefore imagine what could happen if we decide for one option. What will my life look like if I move to St. Gallen, start an apprenticeship as an architectural draftsman, or quit my job as a school principal? Since we don't know what the future will be, we mobilize our imagination. Often, the different options compete in our minds. Which idea prevails often depends on a random intuition. Example: He had to choose between two jobs. One job was at his place of residence, well paid, easy to reach, but moderately interesting. The other job was less well paid but more unconventional. Which one should he choose? As he stood at the station near his residence, a train composition, consisting of old carriages, crossed the track. The train was going to the city of the low-paid job. He looked at the carriages and saw in his mind's eye newspapers offered on hangers at the seats. A few days later, it was clear to him which job he would choose: the lower-paid but unconventional job. The imagination he had at the station helped him to decide.

The contents of our imaginations are often incomprehensible. Why do I fantasize that a water tunnel has been excavated under the river of my town? Why am I obliged to take an exam during a bus ride? Why do I fantasize about blowing up houses in the city center? Often the images contain a meaning that waits to be revealed. The unconscious presents us a mental task. The meanings of images are often difficult to uncover because our thinking and reflecting are more complicated than we subjectively perceive. What we imagine originates in an inner mental underworld for which we lack language and terminology. Our comprehension is limited because we are used to understanding our existence with the lexical-conceptual patterns our culture that we personally have attained. Our perception and understanding are a result of the culture we belong to and our personal history. We acquire the knowledge and mental patterns we need in order to survive in the surroundings into which we are born. We need to adapt. Culture determines what is considered intelligent and which competencies are important. We are considered intelligent if we meet these specifications. In Central European cultures, these are language ability — the more academically you can express yourself, the smarter you are — flexibility in dealing with the standards and codes of the various subgroups, empathy, and perhaps the ability to perform. We are considered intelligent if we can juggle current knowledge, reflect the mainstream, and are flexible in social behaviour. Cultural comparisons show that we humans have more abilities than a single culture can identify and pass on. Our sense of smell could be more sophisticated, our memorising ability greater, our intuition more pronounced, and bodily sensation more holistic. Cultures reflect a percentage of the human abilities. Intelligence is therefore a matter of adaptation within the culture we live. We think according to the specifications of our respective cultures. If we take cultures as reference values, then we might be stupid and clever at the same time, depending on the compatibility. Most of our conscious thoughts are adaptations to our own culture. We move in the linguistic-spiritual context marked out by our culture.

This limitation is necessary because too much insight and knowledge would render us incapable of action, and we would become confused. A view beyond the thinking horizon we are embedded in could unsettle us. Imaginations, like dreams and certain bodily sensations, announce realities *beyond* our range of thought. What we comprehend confirms our habitual positions. Imaginations are therefore also the chance to grasp our being on a deeper level and expand our knowledge. We receive information about psychic processes that are beyond our consciousness and the culture patterns with which we identify. We might gain insights into the depths of our psyche and discover interconnections we have never thought of. This knowledge is transcendent, that is, beyond our linguistic-spiritual view of the world. Imagination therefore stimulates us to think further, deeper, and question habitual positions. They are the starting point of our creativity.

Images promote imagination

Imagination often creates images that are highly suggestive. They then dominate our emotional mood. The effect is strongest when they contain collective, familiar symbols. They are convincing because they arouse or contain emotions. A scenario is presented that adds a new dimension to our existence. Such imaginings might result in changes of routines, encourage us to break rules, or disregard conventions. We might be influenced by a histrionically charged wave. Examples include collective calls for action against global warming. Warnings are backed up with images of sinking Pacific islands like Nauru, desertification in the Sahel, and the melting of the polar ice caps — potent images that make the effects of global warming imaginable.

Do imaginations lead to disappointments?

Imaginations are created in a mental space disconnected from reality. Often, they relate scenes that will never be rehearsed. Sometimes we try to execute an imagined undertaking, but then reality strikes. Two youngsters set out from home, equipped with sleeping bags, a tent, and water bottles. They wanted to experience wilderness. They imagined how they would listen to the trees rustling, discover a fox, have a talk by the fire, before they would snuggle into their sleeping bags. They sought out a forest near their home. Later in the evening after dark, they returned to their parents in panic. The wonderful summer weather had been followed by rain. They had not expected dirty forest floors and getting soaked!

Convincing imaginations can lead to rash decisions. One succumbs to the fascination of a fantasy without carrying out a reality check. A psychologist quit her job as a lecturer at a university, was fed up with internal politics, obnoxious students, and the administrative load with which she had to deal. She imagined an easy and "cool" life on a Greek island. She quit her job, vacated her apartment, and bought a one-way ticket to Greece, where she took over a bar on an island. She relinquished her regular income and benefits to live an island dream instead She was confronted with reality when a bartender ran away with the weekly earnings, the quality of the bar was lousy, and tourists were torturing her with their demands. Some imaginations are hilarious. A teenager who saw me regularly decided he wanted to change the world and start a revolution. He imagined being the chief initiator, a rebel. In order to gain attention and convince people of his vision, he walked up escalators in the opposite direction. He wanted to shock his fellow human beings through his behaviour. Needless to say, his urban guerrilla tactics were not successful. The behavior of the psychologist, the youngster as well as the young man, was based on ideas. These were so powerful that they tried to lead their lives according to their imaginations. They blocked out reality.

Imaginations enrich relationships

Relationships thrive on imaginations. Interestingly, it is more likely that they emerge when we are irritated, worried, delighted, angry, or annoyed. We get emotional and try to understand what is going on. The starting point might be that we are estranged from a friend, got into an argument with a colleague, fell in love, or quarreled with our parents, or are bullied at work. Since everyone ticks differently and no one is programmed by a chip, we are confronted with puzzles. When we fail to understand the behaviour or mood of a person close to us, we start to fantasize. We search for reasons, be it the person's history, background, or in ourselves. In our heads, we reconsider the situations we experienced with him or her, consider his or her background and hope to identify an unfortunate situation or drastic event. The past becomes the sounding board for our guesses. We attribute a colleague's stinginess to his childhood poverty or a friend's self-centeredness to her parents' pampering. We try to identify plausible causes and logical reasons. We want to put the strange behaviour of the colleague or friend into a context that makes sense. We write or fantasize a story that soothes us and puts everything in perspective. These rewrites are rarely factual accounts, but a mixture of reality and fantasy. We develop a convenient story because we are trying to find an explanation for a problematic behaviour. These stories might help us to deal with a fellow human being, a collective phenomenon, a problem, and most importantly, ourselves. It is easier to live with ourselves when we have appropriate stories for our weaknesses and failures. Such stories give us the strength to accept our problematic behaviour and come to peace with odd fellow human beings. "Her aggression is a result of her difficult relation with her father"; "he behaves like a prince because he was overindulged by his parents"; or "he cannot control his temper because his father was serving in the army and has not overcome either the defeat or the atrocities done by the Nazi regime."

The danger of rigid attributions and loss of reality.

The stories we imagine can have problematic effects. This happens often in families. Nobody can choose his or her family members. The result might be that entirely different personalities are confronted with each other. Family members are bound to each other, but at the same time, they might remain strangers. Naturally, this can lead to tensions. In families, one is confronted with the sunny as well as the dark characteristics of the personality. The mutual reproaches can be fierce. One is annoyed by the sheer egoism of the father or irritated by the infantile behaviour of a sister. Relationships within a family are hard work because members cannot avoid each other. The majority of conflicts do not lead to a break-off, but rather one remains in contact and has to endure the others. One must develop a strategy to survive or at least get along with parents, siblings, and spouses and keep up a loving relationship. Often a story is developed about the person in question to make his or her behaviour understandable and acceptable. The story helps us to blend out features or a behaviour that otherwise would trouble us and endanger the relationship. Family members reason that the father cannot express his feelings because he is enormously challenged in his work and had a very difficult childhood, or the mother drinks too much because she feels she is not appreciated and has not overcome her divorce. Such stories help family members live with each other. They serve an important purpose: They enable us to reconcile with fellow human beings who otherwise would annoy, anger, or puzzle us. As with all stories, some parts are true, but many scenes and attributions are fabricated. One reframes the irritating behaviour with the help of a story that captures and explains the causes of the conflict or estrangement. We create stories so we can understand, tolerate, love, work with, or distance ourselves from our fellow beings. Such stories become problematic though when they result in rigid attributions or are too rosy.

Imaginations also influence everyday casual encounters. In both professional and private life, we may associate a person with an unconscious fantasy. I am not talking about prejudices, which are generated by society and help us to cope with numerous contacts. Some encounters activate a complex. A person triggers a sensitive topic in us. Our conscious, rational attitude breaks down, and emotions and images overwhelm us. A story takes hold of us. We start imagining. This happens to us especially with repressed or amoral issues. "When I saw her on the bus, I knew I had to meet her," an architect tells me as part of a project on anima experiences. In his imagination, he was in heaven making love with her. His fantasies overwhelmed him. Finally, he gets to know her, and an affair becomes probable. He is exhilarated, full of expectations as they might at his place. The tension is high as they are about to get intimate. However, when she undresses, he discovers a mole on her back with a hair sticking out of it. From one second to the other, the magic is gone. The fascination has vanished, he has lost his interest in her completely. The woman was a projection carrier for an unconscious fantasy. She triggered his imagination. Such frenzies happen with people who make a godlike impression on us: anima-figures.

Our past: fantasy or fact?

The recollections of our past can never be evidence-based. When we recall our past, we enrich our memories and omit embarrassing things. The scenes we reenact in our heads are based on concrete events but often quotes from what we heard from people close to us. We steal from the experiences or reminiscences of a brother, a sister, or a good friend. In retrospect, we claim it was our experience. We can no longer distinguish between the images that arose in us while listening to an account by a person close to us, a casual encounter, or even a television commercial. Our imagination thus amends or distorts our past with juicy stories and dramatic scenes. Often we revel in deeds we never performed and recount incidents we did not experience. Overall, our pasts are never as dramatic and extraordinary as our soul wishes them to be. Naturally, the dull, banal, and tedious moments outnumber the amazing events. We therefore supplement our past with additional elements of suspense and tune in with extraordinary or publicized events that happened. We are convinced that we were in New York when 9/11 happened, visited the Woodstock festival in 1969, or were a rebellious student. Our descriptions often contrast with reports from contemporaries. "I was an impossible student! I drove teachers mad!" recalls a good colleague of mine. His descriptions stand in stark contrast to mine. I recall him being a well-behaved and obedient student. He rushed home after school and refrained from joining us in events where minor drugs might be involved, not talking about all-night parties or demonstrations, unlike me. Imagination plays tricks on us because it scrupulously quotes from the collective memory, irrespective of its original resource. We steal other people's events and construe what is missing. What really happened cannot be sufficiently be determined in retrospect.

Imagined personality traits

Imaginations influence us when we describe our personality traits.[18] Our self-image is upgraded. We are convinced we are not aggressive or a good team player, although colleagues state the opposite. "My ability is I can listen to other people patiently for hours!" a student's mother informed me after she had bombarded me for over an hour with trivia. I was unable to interrupt her. But, she was convinced she is an excellent listener. Delusional self-appraisals might be irritating for listeners, but psychologically, they serve a purpose. They are important as ego-boosters. We improve our self-esteem. When reflecting on personality traits, men tend to overestimate the importance of their actions or consider themselves more independent than they are, while women overestimate their empathy and social skills. Often, we unconsciously choose lighthearted social occasions for exercises in self-appraisal. Casual, superficial contacts on the internet are also an opportunity to boast and improve our self-esteem. We portray our lives in vivid colors, full of fun and adventure, even if we are sitting alone at home, desperately hoping someone calls us. Often, we hope to increase our social value by boosting our self-image, but many times it is just us we are trying to convince. It becomes problematic when we start believing in the portraits we convey about ourselves.

The media staging of our uniqueness

Our tendency to deceive ourselves is reinforced by modern media. On Instagram, Facebook, or Tinder, we present ourselves as we aspire to be. Teenagers, but also adults, pose in an original or unusual setting, or mime exuberant cheerfulness. Aging men like to post pictures of their sports achievements, be it a marathon or a daring bike tour. On the chosen pictures, they beam sweaty into the iPhone, signaling vitality, success, and pure enjoyment of life. Internet platforms aimed at a virtual circle of friends thrive on the power of imagination. As with small talk or superficial social contacts, they reflect fantasies that are at odds with reality. In larger communities or a business setting, this may well be customary. Political issues, delicate topics, or personal weaknesses are carefully avoided. In order to converse, we have to mask ourselves.[19] Conflicts are dodged, and in-depth talks are considered inappropriate. The art is to master as many contacts as possible without revealing personal traits.

Life is more exciting in foreign places!

Other venues for imaginations are foreign and exotic places and countries. A country or place one is related to becomes an attractive alternative for one's own existence. This often happens when growing up in two cultures. One culture serves as a projection carrier for wishes, dreams, and ambitions. The danger is that one culture is romanticized and the other is rejected. "In Buenos Aires, life is much freer, people there are spontaneous, and, unlike us sober Zurichers, they approach you and radiate warmth!" This was the account of a Swiss youth. He claimed that he could no longer bear the Swiss mentality and insisted on moving to be with his uncle in Argentina. There, everything is different, people are easygoing, sponta-neous, cool, and open. His descriptions were projections, triggered by his

Argentine mother. He himself hardly knew the city and spoke only a few words of Spanish.

One-sided ideas about a country to which the family has a connection are common. The country or city is chosen to place the fantasies. The alternate home or a less familiar place becomes the object of imagination. Fantasies that would remain unconscious manifest themselves. These cities or countries therefore become venues for imaginations, even if there not exotic. The fantasies allow a glimpse into our psyche though.

Does efficiency kill imagination?

Fantasies and escapism do not belong to the standard equipment of coping with the challenges of life. We certainly don't expect these competencies to belong to efficient, successful citizens. Especially when we lead a busy life, have to perform, respect political correctness, woke-ness, and focus on preset goals we have difficulty accessing unconscious fantasies. When our agenda is full and we rush from appointment to appointment, there is not a lot of time for imagination. We adapt to the codes and norms of our social environment. We might even become adherents of our sociocultural environment. Our ideas and conclusions are made in the handwriting of our society, functionaries. We suppress unusual, bizarre, and inappropriate fantasies. They are censored.

Still we believe we are masters of ourselves. In the last pages, however, I tried to expound that the influence of unconscious processes on us is big. They exercise their power in many ways by distorting our past, inventing justifications for our actions, judging relationships, or inter-vening in superficial social contacts and travel decisions.

Our ability to distance ourselves from inner processes is what makes us successful. When we pay no attention to our inner life, we find it easier to cope with social and professional expectations. We are not distracted by inner impulses; instead we concentrate on our conscious competencies and conform to the codes of our social environment. We are usually not aware that we become inept psychologically and maybe even lose contact with ourselves. As long as everything goes well and we comply with societal expectations and our own demands, it does not matter. We function and fit in. Deeper thoughts about ourselves are inappropriate and might even be considered as a sign of weakness.

Even when we are invited during a creativity seminar or a therapy session to let our thoughts float and concentrate on inner images, we tend to recycle our recent thoughts and impressions. The confrontation with the contents of our unconscious averted because our attitude, what Freud called the superego, does not allow it. We don't have any direct access. When the troubles and strifes of our daily life dominate, digging in the unconsciousness is not on the agenda.

The problem is, however, that we cannot avoid ourselves. What goes on inside us influences us, even if we consciously distance ourselves from these autonomous forces. Even when we are convinced that we are in complete control and our actions and words are based on careful and rational deliberations, we might still be distracted or even steered by inner motives. The norms we identify with cannot always be enforced according to our will, because our soul interferes by starting us to imagine.

Our personal autonomy — an illusion?

On the last pages, I tried to describe the influence imaginations have on us, even if we do not perceive them consciously. To function, however, we must be convinced of the autonomy of our own thought processes. Therefore, we understand what is going on in our head as independent acts. We think and then act accordingly. Subjectively, we are convinced that our actions are the result of rational thoughts. We do not acknowledge the influence of fantasies because this insults the image we have of ourself. We are being; we are in command of ourselves!

However, imagination is a core competence. We probably imagine constantly. However, it is difficult to acknowledge the influence of imagination in our daily lives. Imaginations do not determine our actions and decisions, but they influence our goals and thoughts. They present themselves via visions, such as the one which drove Worsley, influence small talk, shape our presence on the internet, expand our personal histories, manipulate decisions and conversations, create speculations about the past and help draw future visions. In the threshold between conscious and unconscious, things express themselves for which we often cannot find adequate words or understanding.

The power of imagination reveals itself regularly when we are confronted with existential decisions, e.g., the purchase of a house, the choice of a profession or partner, the founding of one's own company. The more drastic the event, the more we rely on imagination to overcome ambivalence and gain energy. We rarely decide on essential issues on the basis of rational considerations, but we hope to get energized by inner images. When the decision is associated with an attractive image, then it is easier to act accordingly. The inner image provides us with the necessary energy. The ability to imagine is vital.

Mythodrama is a method by which we gain access to imagination, and thus our unconscious, without getting rid of the adaptation mode. As rational thinking is not discarded, it is less likely that we feel ashamed. We include and consider psychic material without requiring a special setting. Mythodrama differs from psychodrama, developed by Moreno. Although Moreno originally also pointed to the imaginary behind everyday actions, psychodrama tends to focus on personal narratives. Psychodrama sessions begin with the personal experiences and problems of the participants. However, in my experience, if personal issues and narratives are the starting point of a group session, then there is a danger of conformity. Since we want to protect ourselves from being scrutinized by others, we naturally modify our issues according to the perceived expectations of the other participants. In order not to lose our face, for reasons of loyalty or because we fail to find the right words, we present ourselves according to the expectations of the group. In order to be on the safe side, we sometimes even recap topics offered by mainstream psychology: experiences of sexual molestation or abuse; sufferings because of uncaring parents; incidences of bullying in school or at work. We avoid relating shocking, unflattering, embarrassing, or denigrating experience because we are ashamed. Hardly anyone would admit to an attempted rape, a vicious lie or a systematic abuse of a partner to the members of a group session.

However, when we use stories, our self-imposed mental-linguistic corset might crack. A story might present a disruptive moment into a group. The story then helps the participants to lay down their self-imposed reservation and explore new inner territories. It helps to see current concerns, sensitivities, fears, and complexes from another perspective. When the participants in a group imagine being part of the story, they adopt ideas of the protagonists and imagine an event that they have not experienced themselves. Their imagination is activated. The stories become an opportunity to tap into inner resources and gain new ideas. Behavioural options are presented in the images evoked by the story. For example, if someone fantasizes that, thanks to a special jumping technique, the protagonists of a story hop from stone to stone and thus escape from the island to the mainland, then perhaps this added scene indicates that agility, a safe ground, and being focused are important to overcoming a current challenge.

As described in chapter 4.4, the stories in Mythodrama do not contain an explicit moral message. They relate extraordinary events and include mental movers. Such stories might have an impact, trigger feelings, and finally help generate new ideas. The participants renounce their adaptation mode and connect with personal resources. Mentally, they move into a realm where anything is possible, including the opposite. Their imagination is awakened and seizes the scepter. Since their story does not convey a moral message, the chances are that the listeners won't abide the main-stream opinions and social expectations. They allow themselves to consider new, unusual options. their creativity is awakened.

Between reality and fantasy: Children and imagination

Children's development depends on their ability and willingness to imagine. During their development, children and adolescents develop many fantasies on what they will do when they reach adolescence. They create scenes and give themselves roles and challenges. They live in their own world. These are often unrealistic. They envisage themselves being captain of a cruiser, dream of being a pop star or the richest man in the world. What they imagine and the goals they set themselves are often unrealistic, but that is not the point. The purpose of these fantasies is to give children or adolescents hope and the energy they need to keep going and continue their personal development. Many children and adolescents derive current goals from imaginations. They make an effort at school because they imagine themselves living in a house with a pool one day, traveling the world as a famous soccer player. Such images strengthen them so they can cope with problems and challenges in school and in conflicts. Much like Worsley, they align themselves with an image that gives them the energy they need to meet demands. If we want to help children in their development, then we should include their need for imagination in teaching and education.

ENDNOTES

[1] T.H. Huxley, *Evidence as to Man's Place in Nature.*

[2] C. Darwin, *The Origin of Species.*

[3] A.R. Wallace, "On the law which has regulated the introduction of new species," *Annals and Magazine of Natural History*, Vol. 16 (2nd Series), September.

[4] T. Suddendorf, *Der Unterschied – Was den Menschen zum Menschen macht.*

[5] M. Konner, *The Evolution of Childhood.*

[6] U. Schiefele & I. Schreyer, Intrinsische Lernmotivation und Lernen, *Zeitschrift für Pädagogische Psychologie*, 8,1-13.

[7] J. Haidt, *The Happiness Hypothesis*, p. 69ff.

[8] E.H. Shackleton, *The Heart of Antarctic.*

[9] V. Kast, *Imagination als Raum der Freiheit.*

[10] J.G. Fichte, *Grundlage der gesamten Wissenschaftslehre als Handschrift für seine Zuhörer.*

[11] J. Schulte-Sasse, Einbildungskraft/Imagination K. Barck, M. Fontius, D. Schlenstedt, B. Steinwachs & F. Wolfzettel (Eds.), *Ästhetische Grundbegriffe*, p. 128.

[12] J.J.B. Morgan, *Child Psychology*, pp. 215ff.

[13] J.L. Singer & K.S. Pope, *The Power of Human Imagination.*

[14] L. Reddemann & J. Stasing, *Imagination*, p. 13.

[15] L. Reddemann, *Imagination als heilsame Kraft.*

[16] H. Leuner & E. Wilke, *Katathym-imaginative Psychotherapie.*

[17] T. Sodendorf, *The Gap: The Science of What Separates Us from Other Animals.*

[18] J. Haidt, *The Happiness Hypothesis*, p. 69ff.

[19] E. Goffmann, *The Presentation of the Self in Everyday Life.*

6

Implementation of Inner Images

Summary

This chapter describes how the contents of imaginations are processed and used therapeutically. The fantasies of the children or adolescents are not only discussed, but also expressed pictorially or dramatically so that outsiders can guess what was going on inside them. Methods such as drawing, role play, and dramatization are introduced to the group participants so the fantasies become tangible. They serve subsequently as the starting point for new ideas and help the children and adolescents think of concrete conclusions for their questions and problems.

The light switches on and illuminates the room. One boy rubs his eyes, another lies on a mattress pretending to sleep, while a girl sits upright and giggles as she watches two boys poke each other. Some children imagined how the story might continue and are eager to relate their version, two children did not manage to focus on inner images, and one boy got so relaxed that he fell asleep. This is a typical situation after children or adolescents have done some imagination. After they have finished, they report back in their own way. Their task is not to express the scenes they imagined. They might draw a picture, develop a play, or talk about what was going on in their heads. Expressing and reflecting on the contents of the imagination is the core task of the fourth phase of Mythodrama. When the children or adolescents present pictures or create a play based on their fantasies, this group leader might gain some insight into what is going on inside them. The group leaders can help the children or adolescents to develop new ideas in coping with their respective problems. As mentioned in the last chapter, the imaginations are an important source for new approaches in coping with the respective problems of the children or adolescents or the group.

Pictorial representation of the contents of the imagination

One method is to offer the children or adolescents an unlined sheet of A3 paper, a box of colors and invite them to draw their conclusions. We ask them to focus on their own continuation. They need not reproduce the whole story. This must be explicitly told to the children or adolescents, otherwise they tend to draw the whole story and by that avoid personal issues. The scenes they have fantasized might be relevant for further therapeutic work. Depending on the degree of restlessness and tendency to imitate each other, the Mythodrama leader must remind the group members not to interfere with each other's drawing. When a participant is a talented in drawing, there is a danger that the others copy the picture. He or she impresses the less talented ones with his or her drawing skills. However, this is not about drawing talent but about symbolizing psychic inner life. Drawing skills often even limit the authenticity of the pictorial expression. The Mythodrama leader therefore also tells the group that the quality of the pictures is of no significance. It is therefore not necessary to have a talent for drawing or to enjoy drawing to express one's own conclusion pictorially.

Some children also fall back on stencils that they have acquired or developed themselves. They reproduce patterns they are well-acquainted with. They might understand, for example, how to sketch ships with few strokes or how to depict a character in a comic-like way. The danger is that the other group members imitate their template. Mutual influence is basically unproblematic and a sign that the group members are responsive to each other. However, the goal of mythodramatic group work is to encourage group members to develop personal representations of their inner worlds.

Instead of ballpoint pens, we hand out wax crayons. They have proven to be the best in creating the pictures because they have a strong opacity.

The advantage is that their stroke is broad, pasty, and slightly smudgy. There is less danger of getting lost in the details. This increases the likelihood that emotions will be expressed through the different print thicknesses.

The children or young people must be given enough space on the sheet to realise their ideas. However, the drawing sheet must not be too large or too small. The children should not lose themselves on the sheet but perceive it as a set and limited space. Thanks to the limitation of the space, the painters are more likely to connect the individual elements of their drawings. This results in an overall concept. We distribute even larger sheets when a subgroup draws the conclusion of the story together. Two or four children then have the task of telling each other their endings, agreeing on a common conclusion before starting with the picture. This approach is chosen when the focus is on an issue the whole group shares rather than concerns of individual children. It may be about group dynamics or a problem that is on everyone's mind. This approach is chosen in interventions in school classes but also in thematic therapy groups. For example, if the story is about visits to the other parent, the children will inevitably bring in their experiences and share them with the subgroup. When they discuss their conclusion later, they transfer the solutions they fantasized in their story endings to their life. Their common ending contains coping strategies that they can employ in their personal lives.

For example, in a final version in a group for children of divorce, the protagonist of the story covered his ears. He refused to hear the content of his parents' brawls. The boy, who invented that ending presented his version to his colleagues. His version expressed a strategy that children often choose when they can't cope with their mother's or father's accusations about their ex-partner. Picturing this response facilitated the children's conversation about this problem. They shared the conclusion of their group member and then moved on to discuss other possible reactions. Consciously, they were focusing on the story, but actually they were talking about themselves. Concentrating on the story allowed them to reveal own fears, hopes and discuss solutions. Agreeing on a common conclusion in the subgroup and then drawing it together is recommended in ongoing Mythodrama groups.

To enable the group members to concentrate on themselves and not get distracted, they should keep enough distance from each other. Therefore, before the story is related, we ask the children or adolescents to keep their distance. If they are lying on the floor, they should be able to row their arms and legs without touching another group member. If the children or young people are sitting or lying too close to each other, then there is a risk they engage in some social interactions, like giggling, poking at each other, or starting to talk.

Interpretations

Pictorial representations facilitate access to the content of the imaginations. However, it is not only about the reproduction of the imagined stories. The hands of the children or adolescents are also led by unconscious ideas and emotions. The drawings therefore reveal emotions, issues, and experiences of which the children or adolescents are not aware. They reflect sensitivities, moods, and complexes. What preoccupies children or adolescents is indicated by the choice of objects, the design of the space, the colors, the composition, the strength of the stroke, the attention to details, and in the outcome of the story. In spontaneous drawings, we cannot avoid imparting our themes. They express themselves in a coded way. To discern a deeper meaning, we need to interpret the representations. Our task is to connect the content of the picture to unconscious issues of the child or adolescents or the group.

Drawings never capture inner images accurately. The pictures or dramatizations of the stories have to be considered distorted representations of the imaginations. Also, the content and mode of representation of imagined scenes change during the act of drawing. Situational factors that the draftsperson is exposed to during drawing have an impact on the picture, too.

The approach the Mythodrama leader chooses when he is studying the content of the picture is decisive. It's not about finding truths, dirty secrets, or hard facts about the lives of the children or adolescents; neither is he or she searching for proof of traumatic experiences. The main goal is to enlarge one's perspective. He or she is searching for ideas to understand the background and context of the children's or young people's challenges. The Mythodrama leader assumes that the pictures contain information he has not retrieved yet. The pictures are full of secrets that have not been told. The Mythodrama leader works hermeneutically, understanding the image as the expression of a meaning to be inferred. To discern this meaning, one must go through a process: allowing associations, consulting symbolic knowledge, making connections, and hypothesizing. It is therefore important that the Mythodrama leader perceives himself or herself as a facilitator who remains curious. The leader interprets the images on the principle that the drawings contain clues to the emotions, injuries, and expectations of the children or adolescents. However, he or she is not looking for evidence but for insights to better understand the child or adolescent in question.

When we socialize, we present ourselves to our fellow humans. We reveal emotions, traits, and complexes without consciously realizing it. Everything the children or adolescents do or say contains messages about their personality. When we interpret, we try to retract this information. As the contents are not explicitly formulated, we need to try to decipher the hidden messages. This is the perspective we need to choose when we approach the objects and figures that children or young people include in their pictures. When we interpret pictures or dramas, we need to distance ourselves from a rational way of thinking and reasoning based purely on facts. It is not facts we are searching for, but clues about their psyche that we intuitively might discover. We approach the products of the children or adolescents with the assumption that additional information might be available with help of the pictures or dramas. It is more probable that this information reaches us when we have an understanding of symbols. We put aside previous conclusions and try to be open to new insights. Even if the drawings seem to repeat the dynamics of the story or seem ordinary, they might carry statements about the children or young people and their mental processes: The outlined landscapes, the sketched figures, and the chosen objects are not accidental. For example, if a child draws a red sports car, this might be a hint to aggression, machismo, sexual energy, or prestige.

However, our conclusions should be verified or falsified in dialogue with the drawer. Symbols are ambiguous and vary in meaning depending on personality and the knowledge of the interpreter. An object might reflect our biography or the sociocultural context to which we belong. A tree is a symbol of life and personality, but the tree of an individual child might have yet another meaning The tree may then be charged with additional personal meanings: It may be associated with a grandparent's garden, where one can hide in the crown of a tree, or recall an accident in which a family member was killed by a tree. While for one person's airplanes are associated with a sense of freedom and crossing boundaries, another person identifies in them a symbol of pollution. Symbols have collective as well as individual meanings.

Searching for symbolic messages in the actions, words, drawings, and body sensations is of prime importance in therapeutic work. We gain a deeper understanding of a fellow human being when we relate his or her actions and our impression of him or her to possible motives, his or her biography and social context.

Our consciousness discerns only a small part of what concerns and bothers us. We are never aware of everything that is going on inside us or that burdens us. Consciousness must be perceived of as a cone of light in a dark room. The illuminated spot lets us identify only a small part of what can be found in the room. Especially unpleasant, amoral, and burdensome topics remain in the dark. To function in everyday life, they must be omitted. Therefore, our conscious point of view may not recognize all the dramas that take place in the inner world. However, when we draw, our hand is guided by our overall personality. Drawings therefore contain more information than we suspect. They express sensitivities, fears, traumas, and resources that are not familiar to us as drawers.

The interpretations serve as a bridge to the inner world and personality. Crucial in this interpretive work is the attitude of the therapist. His or her interpretations are an attempt to understand what is going on in the child or adolescent. He or she understands this as a tentative approach to the psychic reality of the child or adolescent; he or she is not looking for proofs. The conclusions in Mythodrama are therefore hypotheses or mental movers. As therapists, we try to broaden our view and develop new perspectives. We do not claim supremacy; instead, we make subtle suggestions. These are brought forward playfully in order to recognize blind spots or to gain new insights. The therapist is not the one who knows but merely the person who points out something so it can subsequently be analysed.

Many drawings seem easy to understand, while some remain perplexing. A girl draws a self-portrait. The moment she finishes she does not put the pencil aside but destroys what she did with a few heavy strokes. The message seems clear: identity crisis, self-hatred. Or, a boy's house is surrounded by a big, guarded wall. In his case, too, the message seems obvious: no entry, he wants to protect himself and is afraid of attacks. Some pictures are more puzzling. When a child draws a group dancing around a fire and one recognizes a sheep in the background, then different conclusions are possible. The image might express a need for connection to a community. The fire suggests passion. The community joins for a dance, striving for a rapturous state. Maybe the drawer wants to forget and connect with fellow human beings. The dance around the fire might signify sharing passion. The image might concur with Celtic fertility rituals, wherein people dance around a fire to celebrate life and fertility.[1] The sheep in the background may signify docility or perhaps sacrifice. Sheep blindly join a group, do what they are told. When a child or adolescent draws such a picture, it is a resource for metaphors that help you understand the child's psyche. Community, passion, sacrifice, docility may be terms by which one can approach the child. On the basis of interpretations, we can formulate theses about the state of mind of the child or adolescent.

Misconceptions and false conclusion are possible when interpreting a picture. Because symbols are ambiguous, they allow for different interpretations. The danger is that we project a statement into a drawing that does not correspond to the person who drew it. We impute a motive, need or problem to the child or adolescent. As an interpreter, one has to be alert:

We are never 100 percent sure whether what we conclude is correct or even relevant. Our deliberations might reveal an unconscious issue or feeling, but it is also possible that we are projecting a personal theme into the image. Because of the danger of misinterpretation, many psychologists and psychotherapists understandably refrain from interpretations. It is better to say nothing than to impute something to the patient.

We must remember, though, that interpretation is essential for psychotherapeutic work. The reason is that our psyche expresses itself indirectly. Only if we dare to interpret the products of children and adolescents do we have a chance to recognize deeper motives, complexes, or feelings. Thanks to the interpretations, our work gains depth and becomes relevant. If we do without them, psychotherapeutic work remains on the surface. If concrete and explicit statements and declared motives are the basis of our work and we do not search for hidden issues, then we ignore the various layers and complexity of human psyche. If we do not dare to interpret, then we give up a set of tools that are commonplace in everyday life and indispensable in social and professional life. Life is full of riddles and clues we have to decode. For example, if someone tells us that he is feeling fine, but at the same time his voice is trembling and his hands are sweating, we suspect that the statement is probably not true: We interpret! Such thought work is part of human communication and is the basis of empathy. With the help of interpretation, we gain new insights. Without it, we merely confirm what we already know and cement prejudices. When we interpret, on the other hand, we enter new intellectual territory.

Interpretation versus diagnosis

Interpretations must not be confused with diagnoses. Diagnoses describe a condition and identify possible causes. They suggest reasons that lead to a disease or problem. Diagnoses, as listed in the DSM-V, help to systematize disease backgrounds. We tend to forget: They are based mainly on observations and categorized reactions and answers. These observations and findings (symptoms) are then compared with an institutionalised order to identify typical patterns (syndromes). These patterns signify symptom correlations. For example, if someone is coughing, has a fever, and feels bad, they may be suffering from the flu. The cluster of symptoms and findings (results of examinations) is intended to provide insight. We better understand the phenomenon with which we are confronted. A further advantage is that because there is a certain diagnosis, we benefit from the accumulated knowledge about the corresponding disease. We can thus indirectly profit from the experience of colleagues and science. Patients become representatives of the typical patterns, which are described in manuals. We identify the disease or problem and therefore have access to the experience and acquired knowledge gained by fellow professionals working with the psychological problem There is a bigger chance that we propose the correct treatment.

Understanding patients with the help of diagnoses is essential for psychotherapists or psychologists. It signifies the professionalism approach. However, there is a disadvantage. The danger is that a diagnosis leads to a substantification of the mental picture. Our conclusion becomes reality, a thing. One is impressed by the classification system and adopts the corresponding categorization in relation to patients or clients. The therapist does not see in the patient a unique person but places him into a category. The therapist has a "typical ADHD'er" or "bipolar psychotic" and not a personality to be discovered. The danger is that deeper arguments are prevented. We shield ourselves from a deeper, psychological encounter with the patient with help of the diagnosis.

Interpretations, as we handle them in Mythodrama, are not about objectifying a problem but playfully circumventing the patient's issue to gain insights. The interpretations are an invitation to enter an imaginary space. When we fantasise something into the patient by interpreting, the chances are that he or she opens. We connect with the psychic dimensions of the patient. Interpretations therefore often cause astonishment, confusion or consternation, but they can be the beginning for new insights and the key to understanding the inner life.

The setting for interpretations

The way we interpret pictures and dramas depends on the setting of the group. In small groups, the images can be interpreted individually and discussed with the particular child or adolescent, sometimes after other group participants had the opportunity to express their ideas about the particular picture or play. If the group is large and restless, it is advisable to form subgroups. These are also sensible crisis interventions in school. A subgroup consists of no more than five children or youths and is led by a co-leader. It is recommended that subgroups are physically separated. While with children, a leader should be present in each subgroup to guide members; with adolescents or adults, a brief introduction to image interpretation might suffice before the group works on its own. However, experience shows that the results are then less conclusive because most people are not accustomed to carry out interpretations.

Interpretations lay the path for new ideas. Often new questions emerge. However, we should not expect interpretations to deliver clear and precise answers: Interpretation is a method that helps widen our perspective on the issue. They result of an interpretation might often leave us and the drawer bewildered. The reason is interpretations are based on *intuition*, so the conclusions are not clear cut. Furthermore, we approach pictures or objects in a slightly distracted mode. This attitude makes it more probable to discern a message. Too much concentration reduces the scope of possible answers. In the following pages, I will introduce guidelines that can help when interpreting the paintings and the dramas of group members.

It is important to respect the ownership of the pictures done during Mythodrama sessions. Drawings remains private. The Mythodrama leader therefore interprets images only after the drawer has given his or her permission. Above all, the leader does not force any child or adolescent to present his or her picture to the others without his or her prior permission. In practice, however, it rarely happens that someone withholds his or her product. On the contrary, in most of the group sessions, all members desire a comment on their pictures. In order to study a picture and comprehend interpretations, the Mythodrama leader places the picture of the particular group member in the middle of a circle, consisting of the group members or pins the picture on a wall or a flipchart. Before sharing his or her conclusions the leader explains how he or she proceeds. He or she emphasizes that he or she lets himself or herself be guided by the picture when he or she expresses his or her thoughts. The leader points out that he or she is not interested in uncovering dark truths or diagnosing the respective group member; all the leader does is to deliver suggestions. He or she tries to understand the picture from the inside out.

The Mythodrama leader also takes a resource-oriented approach. He or she tries to concentrate on helpful conclusions. He or she is not interested in highlighting weaknesses and uncovering taboos unless it is relevant. The leader's main focus is to develop ideas that help choose a new approach solve the problems of the particular drawer. For example, if a child draws the protagonist of the story standing motionless in front of a ravine, the leader will not conclude immediately that a fatal fall is imminent but will see in the picture an indication that the drawer is challenged and might offer help to overcome a barrier.

Group members may comment on the picture. Again, it is not a question of right or wrong but about collecting ideas. Only after the picture has been interpreted by the Mythodrama leader and the group is the drawer invited to relate his continuation of the story. We ask the group member to withhold his or her version of the continuation of the story because pictures are understood as an *independent* expression of the drawer's state of mind. The explanations of why he or she chose a particular object or scene is often a rationalization. They distract from other messages in the picture. The drawer constructs a rationale for himself or herself because he or she is ashamed of the actual message in the picture or just can't deal with what was expressed. Interpretation is about a verbalization of the impression that the picture conveys to an outsider.

Especially in continuous groups, it is helpful to approach a picture or drama with a specific question in mind. The picture or drama is scrutinized in order to find clues so the question could be answered. Some questions could, for instance, be: How is his or her self-control? What kind of emotions does the picture indicate? Are stresses recognizable? Has the drawer experienced a trauma? How is the quality of the indicated interactions? What expressions do the human figures have? Does the picture convey optimism or pessimism, etc.? Especially in crisis interventions, we consider whether strategies of conflict management are detectable: Weapons might signify bundled aggressions, animals as instinctual forces, interactions as social skills, etc. Hopefully, the interpretations should have an uplifting effect on the children and adolescents and strengthen their self-esteem.

Procedure for interpretations

1) Personal impression: We usually begin interpretations by expressing our spontaneous reactions. We formulate the various ideas that come to our mind when we study the picture for the first time. These comments can be broad and of hand. One might state that the picture reflects a cheerful mode, seems a bit chaotic, contains conflicting elements, has striking colours, etc. However, the leader emphasizes that these are personal comments, that they should not be confused with in-depth interpretations.

2) Dynamics in the picture: Next, the leader focuses on the flow that the picture radiates. He or she tries to discern implied movements. Does the picture make a calm expression? Does a left-right ascending diagonal jump draw one's attention? Does the picture seem weighted? Are there elements confronting each other? Do the dynamics of the picture break the frames of the picture, etc.? The detected dynamics might indicate what is going on emotionally in the child or adolescent.

3) Colours: What colours are chosen is significant. They contain information about the emotional and maybe the attitudes of the drawer. As with all symbols, they might have an individual as well as general significance. Red is associated with life, love, anger, fire, energy, and hate. Red is also the colour of passion. Dark blue we relate to spirit, trust, and compassion. Light blue stands for flexibility, understanding, honesty. Yellow we associate with mind, rationality, spirit, and perhaps ambivalence and happiness. Green symbolises hope, confidence, growth, nature, and harmony. With grey, we might think of stagnation, boredom, restraint, and

unobtrusiveness. White represents innocence, purity, but also sadness. Finally, black is the color of forgetfulness, mourning, and fear. Of course, meanings also depend on the culture. For example, white is the colour of discord in China, but among Hindus, it stands for peace. When attending to the colours of a picture, it is important to try to determine the specific meaning of the colour from the perspective of the drawer and by taking the context into account.

For example, if the drawer uses red to color a human figure and chooses yellow for the roof of the house, then this could indicate that he or she is emotionally connected to a person but ambivalent about how and where the relationship can be lived. The drawer could now be asked which person he or she is emotionally connected to and how the relationship or contact with this person is developing.

4) Composition: The composition that is recognizable in the picture might be interesting and contain clues to the personality of the drawer. Do the elements of the picture relate to each other and to which corner of the picture was the drawer drawn? Very roughly one divides pictures into four equal parts. Each part might signify something. The upper right part might contain some information on the future and ambitions of the draftsman. The right lower quarter, on the other hand, might refer to reality. That corner might indicate how the drawer perceives his own position, The spaces in between might indicate how he or she wants to reach his or her goals. The lower left corner might represent the past. What is his or her perception of his or her origins? The upper left corner may contain hints about the path the drawer intends to choose.

These classifications are not scientifically validated and for many drawings irrelevant. However, the classification can help the viewer understand a picture and extract information about the drawer. We get more creative when we can orient ourselves.

5) Focus: Many children concentrate on one part of the picture while drawing. They invest a lot of energy to one element of the picture. They are more engaged there and use a lot of pressure when drawing lines. As an interpreter, one wants to find out whether this element points to an important issue of the drawer. It might hint to a topic that concerns the

drawer. Some drawers focus on human figures. This indicates a pre-occupation with relationship issues or problems. However, in some pictures, the focus can be discerned in the background; for example, you might see a volcano spewing fire or a man waving on a boat. The focus might be connected with a current, upcoming, or past event. For the interpreter, this means that he or she might have found a clue to what the child or young person is currently most concerned about.

6) Exploiting space: The children are handed a blank sheet. It is interesting how they react to the emptiness of the paper. Do they feel a need to make use of the entire sheet? Do they limit their strokes, concentrate on the middle, and leave a belt of white around the picture, or do they dedicate themselves to another part of the sheet? Some children or young people are not satisfied with the allotted space. They feel the sheet does not offer enough space. What they intend to draw exceeds the sheet they were handed. The house they draw is higher and cannot be represented on the sheet; a forest is wider than the limited space allows; or people they draw seem congested. This might indicate that the ambitions of the drawer are greater than his or her opportunities. However, if there is an abundance of uncovered space, it might indicate a lack of self-confidence. He or she does not dare present himself or herself. The question is also whether the drawer deliberately left some white spaces. Some sketchers paint over all the white spaces. They seem compulsive and seem to detest white. Such overpainting may be a sign of great ambition or perfectionism, or it may be an attempt to exert control. Nothing unexpected is allowed to happen. Most sketchers don't bother, though. The white parts of the sheet seem irrelevant to them. This may be a sign of a certain lightheartedness or perhaps it may indicate carelessness.

7) Content: Only now does the interpreter study the content of the picture. He or she approaches the picture from a different angle. He or she concentrates on the various elements and figures in the picture. He or she perceives them as symbols. They represent something else, an emotion, a thought, or complex of which the drawer is not aware. We therefore try to grasp the deeper meaning that a casually drawn house has, a carefully depicted bus, a nasty snake, or an empty suitcase. Everything that imposes

itself on us as a perceptible object might contain a message. Many meanings are personal and vary from drawer to drawer, though some objects and figures carry cultural meanings. These are shared by the respective group. A tree, for instance, stands for personal development; a car for independence; a policeman for rules or the superego; a lake for feelings, need for rest, introversion or depression; and a flower for hope or beauty. As mentioned earlier, drawn objects usually have different meanings. So, as an interpreter, it is important to evaluate different meanings. What an object symbolises for the drawer should be determined in dialogue with him or her. In many cases, drawn objects have a personal meaning of which we are not aware at first sight. Personal meaning can be detected by talking to the drawer.

8) Conclusion: The seven guiding principles are suggestions on how to approach a picture. How we start depends on the nature and content of a picture. For one child, the colors are important, for another, the spatial design, and for a third, symbol meanings are paramount. The guiding principles help to extract statements from pictures. They are not a guarantee that the conclusions are coherent or valid. The purpose of interpretations is to generate hypotheses.

As mentioned, it is advisable to start with questions. We interpret the picture from a certain perspective: Does it tell me something about the child's state of mind? His or her vision of the future? Most pictures do not provide clear answers to such questions. However, if we approach the images with questions in mind, there is a greater chance that we gain some new information. New ideas might emerge and help to understand the child or adolescent in a different way. The picture gives us a stimulus to think more deeply by broadening our mind.

Dramatization

"We can only fight the curse if we wear two different shoes!" the chief whispers to the prospector, while a robber disguised as a nun sneaks up behind him. However, a dog ambushes the fake nun. When she enters the tent of the chief and the prospector, the dog begins to growl. The dog approaches the fake nun. The chief and prospector are startled. "There!

We've got it . . ." This is part of a drama presented by a subgroup of children as a continuation of a story that takes place on the Orinoco.

Dramatization is another way of implementing the contents, which were imagined. Instead of presenting the conclusion of the story pictorially, the children or young people in subgroups agree on a common conclusion, from which they then create a short theatre. They are invited to perform their dramatized conclusions in front of the other group members. Dramatizations are suitable in therapeutic groups, in school crisis interventions, and in teamwork. Spontaneous acting reveals a lot of our personality. Often the participants disclose aspects of their personalities of which they are not aware. Complexes, emotions, character traits, and personal weaknesses manifest themselves.

It is also telling how players interact with their fellow actors. Patterns are often apparent that are important in order to understand the personality of a particular person. One child suddenly adopts a commanding tone toward his peers, while another stops being a loudmouth and behaves in a humble, reserved manner because he is no longer in the centre, and still another tends to seclude himself. Such observations do not explain the difficulties of the child in question, but they are a piece of the puzzle of the overall picture of him or her. The ways in which players react, choose roles, and perform give us clues about their particular social skills. Moreover, when we perform Mythodramas with teams, the shared conclusions reflect group dynamics and qualities that distinguish the group. I believe it is no coincidence what role the participants choose or are forced to play by the other group members.

In dramatizing the conclusions, the children or youths are addressed as a group. Children must not only verbally agree on a conclusion but interact accordingly during the play. Children or adolescents often don't follow the guidelines they choose for themselves during the dramatizations. Therefore, when they act out the versions they agreed on, surprises are possible: sudden role changes, escalations, or spontaneous rewrites of the previously agreed final version. In a staged shootout, suddenly all group chose to be gangsters; in another play, the two princesses got carried away and started an endless quibble; and in a third play, the child, who's role was a stone revolted and choose to be a magician.

When directing a Mythodrama, you must be ready for such surprises and keep a close eye on the children's or young people's rehearsals. The dramatizations are a concoction of spontaneous theatre and adherence to a discussed script. Role play releases new forces. We experience active imagination. The children or adolescents put themselves into another world, forget about their personae, and slip into roles that might even be alien to them. Role play allows them to distance themselves temporarily from personal difficulties. Stutterers begin to talk normally, shy children approach their peers, and dominant children practice restraint. Role play frees them from constraints, fears, and ambitions. Acting becomes an exceptional experience for many children or young people. Occasionally, an introverted or shy child or adolescent does not seem to profit personally from the theatrical realisation of their imaginary content.

The dramatization of final versions is particularly suitable when a mutual question, problem, or goal is the concern. One focuses on the interests that connect the group members with each other. This is the case in thematically oriented therapy groups: groups for children whose parents are divorcing or separating; groups for children from a parent who struggles with a major psychological problem; groups for children from alcohol-strained families; or groups for young people who have committed a violent crime. In such groups, stories are chosen that reflect their shared experiences. When the children or adolescents subsequently develop the story, they tune in to their common topic both mentally and emotionally. In their dramas, their shared experiences are evident. In school-based crisis interventions, the focus is on the issue that the teachers and parents propose, e.g. bullying, class climate, relationship with the teacher, violence, etc. If a Mythodrama is conducted with a team, then we focus on the agreed topic.

The Mythodrama leader usually decides on the assignment to the subgroups. This procedure is recommended for time reasons. When the children or adolescents are free to choose which group they want to join, this triggers discussions. The children or adolescents attach too much importance to the assignment to the subgroup. They fear that that a nascent friendship won't continue if they are not in the same subgroup with their new friend, or they may not want to reveal their final version of the story to a particular colleague. Thus, the Mythodrama leader decides on the assignment, but it is advisable to take into account the wishes of the children and adolescents and assign the children or adolescents who get along well to the same subgroup. However, this criterion is not communicated to the participants.

In mixed groups, we usually don't insist that each subgroup consist of both male and female members. For school groups and in crisis intervention, the leader lets the students count to three, four, or five depending on the number of subgroups. He then invites the ones, twos, threes, etc., to meet in a designated corner of the room or in separate rooms to form the subgroup.

Before the children or youths disperse, the leader tells them what to do in the subgroup. It is important that he or she gives clear instructions.

Instructions to the subgroups

- Form a circle and then share each other's final versions.

- Alternative: A subgroup sits around a large sheet of paper. Wordlessly, they are then asked to draw their final version together. They may add details to the contributions of the other members of the subgroup. When everyone has finished, the task is to find out which story endings their colleagues have fantasized before discussing and developing a common conclusion. The ending they agree on is then told or presented to the colleagues in the other subgroups.

- When the sharing of the story is completed, the group might want to try to compound a common conclusion — under one condition, though. Their version must include contributions from all group members. One may not take over the version of a participant but must construct a new story using elements from the different final versions of the participants. Everyone must agree with the final version. The group then uses this final version of the story as the base for the drama.

- The roles that are presented in the final version are chosen by members of the subgroup.
- The drama that is developed from the final version should be acted out three to four times.
- All members of the subgroup should participate
- The drama shall be given a title, which will be announced to all.

Additional instructions

Some groups need more guidance. The above instructions will not enable these groups to develop a drama. For such groups, additional instructions can help:

- The theatre that is developed from the final version contains three parts: a beginning, a plot, and a conclusion.
- Each part consists of a specific scene.
- Before presenting the actual play or drama, the children or young people introduce themselves in their roles after one child announces the title of their play.
- Certain catch phrases or poignant remarks are offered that they might want to include in their play. They can consist of sentences like "We know exactly where you have hidden." "We still have the tomatoes to rely on." "If your mother would know." "No, this box is not dangerous."

Requisites

Disguises help children or young people get into the mood for role playing. Their tongues loosen, and they dare to make the odd remark. They gain spontaneity because the mask protects them from immediate criticism and nasty remarks. They overcome their inhibitions because, according to them, they are no longer responsible for their behaviour and words. It is more likely that they reveal their alter ego and become bolder, more spontaneous, more distinct, or the contrary, more shy. In Jungian terms, they are relieved from their persona by masking themselves and presenting their shadow. What it consciously forbidden or taboo can now be expressed. In my work as a group leader in Bern, we had the luxury of having a special dressing room in which the children and young people, once they had agreed on a final version, could choose a disguise that suited their role. We had a wide range of jackets, shirts, jerseys, hats, shoes, suits, pants, and slacks, but also wooden swords, dusters, police hats, helmets, uniforms, toy guns, and dummy rivals. The requisites consisted mostly of donations. When offered such a choice, especially children tend to get excited and create a tremendous mess in no time at all. It is therefore advisable to let one subgroup after the other into the room. They subgroup should wait for its turn. Also, when the children or adolescents change their clothes, a group leader should be present to keep order. Younger children especially tend to rip clothes or other props out of the closets and throw them carelessly on the floor if they don't fit or they don't like them.

Another dress-up option is to put on masks, like the ones you see at Fasnacht or Mardi Gras. Children can then put on an animal mask, turn into a zombie, witch, devil, old man, stern police officer, king, crook, etc. When children or teenagers perform wearing a mask, it might loosen their tongue. However, when the children or teenagers wear full face masks, then they start to sweat with time, when the room is not efficiently ventilated. To prevent sweating, half-face masks, like the ones worn at the Venice Carnival, are convenient. Even though only the eye area is covered, children and young people feel they are somebody else.

If they aren't any props available, then you encourage small changes in clothing. For example, a child might put on a normal jacket or a scarf to give himself or herself a distinct look.

The stage

To perform their final versions, the subgroups need a stage. A stage is defined space in which the dramas take place. The stage does not have to be a conventional stage with curtains and audience area. A defined area of the floor can be sufficient. It can be the back part or an unobstructed area of the therapy room. In school classes we choose the part of the classroom where the class council meetings are held, a gym or the hall, where school meetings are being held.

The role of the group leader during the drama

A Mythodrama leader announces the subgroups. He or she might want to present the subgroup in a slightly theatrical way, acting like a theater director. Of course, he or she emphasizes that the audience, which consists of the other subgroups, will certainly enjoy the exquisite, once-in-a-lifetime performance. The title of the play is stated by either the Mythodrama leader or one of the performers. The Mythodrama leader explains that on his or her clap of the hands, the play begins. When he or she claps twice, the play is over, or everyone on the stage should freeze. Especially if the children or youths are not wearing a costume, it is recommended that they briefly introduce themselves in character and perhaps even bow, as is customary in a real theatre.

After these primary actions the Mythodrama leader declares in a loud and clear voice: "The play begins," and bows. Now it is up to the children or youths to rehearse their final versions. As the reader can imagine, the quality of the plays vary. Often subgroups develop highly original conclusions and impress the audience with their acting skills, other conclusions seem improvised, ordinary, boring, and too provocative. Some subgroups might not stick to their agreed conclusion but get carried away and rewrite their part spontaneously. Their play becomes an improvisation.

The value of the drama does not depend primarily on the acting skills of the children or adolescents. Also, if they don't follow their script, that is not a problem. When a scene develops that previously had not been discussed and the children or adolescents start to improvise, this offers an opportunity to understand them even better. When they improvise, they express candidly what is on their minds. They reveal emotions, anger, and hope. Spontaneous eruptions are more likely if the children or young people know each other. They explored each other's personalities, can fool around with, tease, and provoke each other. Their interactions become chaotic. The result is that hot issues and sensitive topics are no longer taboo. Sexual innuendos, violent fantasies, and obscenities are expressed despite the presence of the leader. Since they have had several sessions together, there is a good chance that a sense of community has developed that tolerates inappropriate expressions. Children who know each other are more likely to gauge the reactions of other participants. One is no longer horrified when a participant uses coarse language or has a proximity-distance problem. Their dramas become more spontaneous. In one-time groups in which the participants are not acquainted, politically incorrect statements, provocative innuendos, and inappropriate fantasies are less likely. The children or young people are afraid to expose themselves and therefore behave.

In one-time groups, there is also a danger that the group leader does not recognize hidden dynamics, bullying, or intrigues because he or she is not familiar with the individual child or youngster. For such groups, therefore, guided, semi structured theatre play is recommended.

Starting off with a script they decided on by themselves helps the respective children or adolescents feel safe. They do not feel that they are exposing themselves, divulging secrets or personal issues. The setting allows them to express their own concerns and show the sensitivities without exposing themselves. Their issues are expressed *symbolically* and dealt with *indirectly*. Subjectively, they are contributing to a story that has been related. This allows them to reveal emotions and challenges without them realizing it. According to their perception, the play is about common conclusions and not about their problems at home, experiences of violence or a bad personal incident.

Feedback and discussion

After a drama, feedback is obtained from the Mythodrama leader and other group members. This is done according to guidelines and under the guidance of the Mythodrama leader. He or she poses specific questions to the audience or performers. It is important that he explains beforehand that the purpose is not to judge, but to give the players food for thought. The feedback should help the players gain new perspectives about themselves. So the leader should not focus on whether the drama was "cool," but on what the game triggers in the participants and audience. Analogous to the feedback in other phases of Mythodrama, one focuses on the *positive* aspects. Thus, the play should not be criticized by the audience and the Mythodrama leader, the idea is to share observations and verbalize conclusions.

Possible questions to the audience are:
- What did you notice?
- What role would you chose for yourself? Why?
- What characteristics do you recognize in the players? Why?
- What kind of present would you give to each of the players?
- What was forgotten in the play?
- Which players belong together?
- What would you do differently in the play?
- What have you already experienced?
- Who is the poorest person in the play?
- How does the play continue?
- Which item do you wish to possess?

Depending on the group constellation, the Mythodrama leader asks these questions and invites the participants to give spontaneous answers, or he or she focuses on individuals. Another possibility is to invite the participants to answer the question for themselves without having to share their responses. In restless groups, however, it may be appropriate to hand out the questions in writing. After the children or young people have answered them, they hand the slips of paper back to the group leader. The leader then perhaps reads them out loud without revealing who has written them. If the answer is addressed to an individual participant, then, of course, the Mythodrama leader hands the answers back to the writer. He or she can decide whether to read his or her answer out loud. As mentioned, the questions should concern the play.

The Mythodrama leader, of course, if he or she thinks it is appropriate, may want to add further questions or make remarks. The participants might form a circle or take a place in the audience or on the floor. The participants then take turns in stepping onto the stage and receive feedback. The Mythodrama leader joins the respective children or adolescents. He or she enters the stage space, puts a hand on a shoulder of the respective child or youngster before posing his or her question or making a remark. Following Moreno's psychodrama, he or she might address the participant in the first-person form. This gesture accents the act. It is important, though, that the feedback or questions not expose or embarrass the child or young person in question. Therefore, the Mythodrama leader emphasizes that the interviewees have the possibility of keeping the answer to themselves. They don't have to communicate them to the others. Children are told to put their hands on their head to signal that they don't want to share their answers. The purpose of this feedback is not an evaluation of the play. The goals is to sharpen the players' perception of themselves or to challenge their own preconceptions. How the feedback is received and whether it has any effect at all is, of course, difficult to distinguish. If a player is told, for example, that he or she seems cheeky and self-confident, she or he may react astonished, be embarrassed, or feel confirmed. Depending on one's own self-image and mood, this remark will trigger a thought process or be ignored.

Possible questions to the children or youths after playing the final version include:

- How did you feel?
- What would you change in retrospect?
- Who was your friend during the play?
- What changed you?
- What ending would you have liked as well?
- Have you also experienced a similar situation?
- What part of the game do you remember? Are you embarrassed by any part of the game?
- Did you get to play what you wanted?

Again, the participants don't have to address the group; they can give the answer to themselves without have to divulge the content.

Responses with cards

Another possibility is to use *cards*. The Mythodrama leader presents the group a choice of cards with pictures that symbolize personality traits. It can be a cell phone, a car, a sweater, a sword, a gun, a shield, a helmet, a megaphone, a spear, a mask, a wooden spoon, a bicycle, a soccer ball, a nice dress, a book, a bed, earplugs, etc. The pictures represent a behaviour or are generally associated with a personality trait.

Mood pictures might also do the trick. Postcards or pictures that express sadness, joy, fear, grief, aggression, happiness, anger, etc., can be found on the internet and printed out. Some pictures might depict scenes: children dancing in a field, a person venturing over a shaky suspension bridge, an impressive waterfall, a road disappearing into the horizon, crossroads, a stormy sea, a rainbow, an abandoned house, a moistened flower, a lonely tree, a child eating ice cream, two children looking happily at each other, a grim clown, a beaming mother, an angry protester, etc. It is important that the images do not reflect too many negative characteristics. The idea is that the group participants choose the pictures, which reflect their mood.

Another possibility is to display several objects that are loaded with meaning. The children or adolescents might then want to choose one to express their mood or the feelings they perceive in a colleague. For instance, marbles might stand for energy or ladybugs for good luck.

Free improvisation of the finale version

Another way to work with the imagined endings is improvisation. After the imagination phase, all group members form a circle. They then share their individual conclusions. After having heard various conclusion, the members of the group choose a role that they heard in the conclusion of someone else or that they chose themselves. The choices are then presented and discussed before proceeding to the introductory scene. The roles can be determined in different ways:
- The group leader paraphrases the roles that appear in the story and the conclusion versions and then lets children choose spontaneously.
- The children or young people indicate which character they want to play.

Whenever possible, the children or youths agree among themselves how to distribute the roles. If two or more group members opt for the same role, then two or even three group members might play the role. However, the group leader makes it clear before the impro-theater begins that it is allowed to switch roles during the play. They Mythodrama leader might make suggestions during the play.

The Mythodrama leader might also use doubling, repetition, order a freeze, or suggest a role reversal. A player might raise his or her hand to indicate that he or she would like to switch or play out a new role. The Mythodrama leader then tells all players to remain still in their respective positions (freeze) so that the player in question can take up his or her new role.

Another way to allocate the roles of the play is to use cards on which the protagonists and antagonists are depicted. Each card represents a character in the story. When participants choose a card, they briefly introduce the character before playing it. Again, instead of cards, items can be presented that distinguish the protagonists and antagonists. If there is a captain in the story, there is a captain's cap on the floor; if there is a soldier, there is a toy gun; if there is a prima donna, there is makeup. Distributing the roles with the help of objects is especially popular with younger children. The participants are asked to think about which role they want to play in the introductory scene.

Now, one must decide what the introductory scene should look like. It is advisable to use elements from all the participants' story ends. This way, they are more likely to identify themselves with the story that delivers the outgoing scene. They made a personal contribution to the improvised drama. To initiate the impro-drama, the Mythodrama leader paraphrases the entry scene and the roles that the children or youths have chosen. The roles can be introduced, as is common in psychodrama, by the Mytho-drama leader standing behind the respective participant and placing his hands on his or her shoulders. He talks in the name of the participant and begins by asking in first person to introduce himself or herself, his or her characteristics, appearance, and role. After everyone has presented his or her role, the drama begins: the final conclusion of the story, which will be developed during the improvised drama.

Willingness to improvise varies from group to group. It depends, among other things, on factors that we can influence to a limited extent:

the group constellation, the spectrum of personalities in the group, the children's image of the group.

One prerequisite for improvisation is that the children or young people know each other well and have a stable relationship with the leader and each other. This is especially the case in therapeutic groups. When the children or adolescents get acquainted with each other over several sessions, there is a greater chance that they will trust each other and open up. They perceive the group as a place where they can express personal thoughts and feelings without being ridiculed, hearing nasty remarks, or being confronted with incredulity. As a rule, mutual trust sets in after at eight to 10 sessions. That is when the group starts to develop impressive and often very original scenes.

In free improvisation, the group leader can proceed according to the rules of drama therapy as described by Aichinger and others.[2] The shared fantasies help the participants engage in the improvised drama. The Mythodrama leader does not have to stand aloof; he or she might also want to get involved. He or she tries to identify the children's or adolescents' concerns and feeling and express them in his or her interventions in a playful way. It can be an issue of the group or an individual player. However, depending on the story, it might be appropriate pick out a role that is not attractive and therefore has been forgotten or avoided. For example, in one story, a snake played an important role. It instilled evil thoughts in the protagonists of the story; or in another story, a stone, which contained secrets and could talk under certain circumstances was in the focus. Not surprisingly, no child picked the role of the snake or the stone. However, according to the group leader, they were important characters in the story. They represented shadow elements. For this reason, he or she decided to represent one of these roles himself.

Conclusion

This chapter is about the representation of the imagined final versions. I tried to explain that there are different approaches on how to implement imaginations. Which one to choose depends on the profile of group, the preferences of the group leaders and, of course, the age and wishes of the children or young people involved. In the dramas, it is important that the children and young people experience and imagine their fantasies. After having them visualized or dramatized, it is easier to refer to and talk about them. Thus, unconscious messages or overseen backgrounds are easier to detect and made conscious. Interpretations based on a picture, drama, or free improvisation provide valuable stimuli that help the children and young people think more deeply about themselves, develop new perspectives, and confront their challenges. The interpretations serve as a bridge between the inner and outer world.

During the free improvisations, the Mythodrama leader keeps the upper hand. He or she comments on individual scenes and supports the children or young people in their play. "So, what does the princess actually think when her prince suddenly takes off in a balloon and calls out Arschguggi?"[3] he or she will say, for example, addressing the princess and thus encouraging her to speak up. However, the leader will also have to give stage directions, clapping his or her hands when he or she wants people to be quiet and listen, giving a signal when the play is over, or taking in the name of a participant. When he or she claps with his or her hands and demands everyone's attention, he or she might want to introduce a new element or figure or make a comment. In one improvisation, the game master announced to the youth that the sheriff is now coming to look for the bad guy. He or she introduced this character because the drama was in danger of flagging.

In our experience, improvisations should not last too long and be distinguishable from the other activities. The leader signals when the improvisation starts and stops. Participants should regard improvisations as a special activity, a phase during which one experiences oneself differently. As in the plays by the subgroups, sometimes disguises help participants to act spontaneously and lose some initial inhibitions.

In one-time groups, in intervention classes, or at story festivals,[4] a more structured approach is appropriate. The children and especially the young people are more inhibited and often hesitant to express personal issues. They fear animosities, conflicts of interest or cynical reactions. Young people whose personalities are in flux tend to compensate for their own insecurities by acting cool or fooling around.

ENDNOTES

[1] A. von Scotti, *Nur Sommer: Irische-schottische Kirche.*

[2] A. Aichinger & W. Holl, *Gruppentherapie mit Kindern. Kinderpsychodrama,* Band 1.

[3] Derogatory term in Swiss.

[4] www.cliqcliq.ch

7

The Step into Reality: the Transfer

Summary

The goal of Mythodrama is to find an answer to an individual problem of a participant or the entire group and then to decide on a concrete change that hopefully will ameliorate the situation. This goal is achieved by employing a specific strategy. The outcomes of imagination and of the subsequent processing phase are connected to the real-life experiences of the participants. Real life means it is not only an issue by which one is personally intrigued, worried, bothered, or annoyed, but is an issue that is of general concern. What others say is also relevant, be it the other group members, the parents, school, the authorities, or foes. After the problem is on the table, ideas for an answer are searched. The conclusion should be based on the produced material. The strategies and solutions that appeared in the drawings, the dramatizations, or conversations render ideas about how to solve the initial problems. The interpretations expressed in the previous phase serve as a resource for new ideas to decide on a concrete change in the daily life of the person or the group.

"Don't we need olives?" the girl asks her colleague in a snooty tone. "Surely not, having enough tomato sauce will do!" the latter replies snappishly, while in the background two colleagues roll out dough and grunt loudly. The scene took place in a school building in Zurich's Glatt Valley. The students in the fifth grade had decided that they would prepare lunch for themselves and the teachers on their own, without any help from adults. The last two school lessons were reserved for this undertaking. The students bought the food, reserved the school's kitchen in the basement, divided the work among themselves and dished up paper plates on tables in the adjoining room of the kitchen. They were in charge of lunch! They had come up with the idea of this project, called "Making a pizza dinner together" in the last phase of the Mythodrama: the transfer. Originally, the teacher had called for an intervention because there was great tension among the students, no sense of community, and individual students were being maltreated. Academic results were in the basement, parent complaints were staggering, and truancies became a real problem. The intervention's purpose was to strengthen the cohesion of this fifth-graders, motivate them to concentrate on learning, and improve collaboration with parents. The intervention consisted of four half-day sessions, during which we worked with the class doing Mythodrama. The youngsters listened to the stories attentively, fantasised about their endings, dramatized the conclusions and discussed different interpretations. Finally, in the last phase of the Mythodrama session, they were asked to decide on a change that would improve their situation and solve some of the problems they were struggling with.

The students were asked by the Mythodrama leader to come up with ideas on how to improve the mood and strengthen cooperation within the class. After intensive discussions, they decided to organize a pizza lunch for themselves and other colleagues. It was important for the class members to do everything on their own. They were responsible. Under no circumstances was an adult allowed to help them. Naturally, there was an initial skepticism on the part of the teachers and some of the parents. Was there a danger of chaos? The teachers discreetly helped, but the students did most of the work on their own. The class members wanted to prove to themselves that they were capable and able to work together. The pizza event was a bit chaotic, but it helped to change the general mood and attitude of the students. They felt that they were not fulfilling the teachers' wishes but doing something on their own. The destructive mood had disappeared gradually and the motivation to attend school increased — even if the quality of the pizza was questionable.

During the transfer phase of the Mythodrama, one concentrates on a concrete change. Before, the group had dived into a world of their own, by imagining, drawing, dramatizing or interpreting the performances. The art is now to extract ideas for concrete change from these fantasized and subsequently drawn or acted story endings. This starts with the theme that was formulated at the beginning of the session by the Mythodrama leader.

The Mythodrama leader accompanies the search for a change and helps with the decision-making process. He or she listens to the participants' proposals, makes notes on a flip chart, poses questions, discusses the chances of realization, and maybe refers to alternative ideas expressed during the editing phase. For the process to produce a useful result, a consistently resource-oriented strategy is useful. The Mythodrama facilitator focuses on the constructive suggestions of the participants. The focus is on what can be done. He or she does not address unrealistic or problematic change proposals. The focus is on suggestions for change that can be derived from the participants' story endings and are feasible. Because the suggestions come from the participants, there is a greater chance that the appropriate change will be adopted and implemented. The chance is that the participants identify with the discussed change because they developed it themselves. In the example above, the children fantasized that the villagers in the story would organize a feast before taking action against an evil alpine ruler who demands child sacrifice.

The changes the individuals or the group decide on should be *concrete*, meaning that the social environment remarks that something decisive has happened. Things are getting better! Proposals that involve a change in the behaviour of others not involved will not be followed up by the leader.

The transfer phase is hard work. After having floated in other worlds, dreamt of fantastic endings, and engaged in plays, the group now faces the reality of their lives. The chatting phase is over. If idealistic solutions are introduced, then the leader tries to establish a connection to reality. So, for example, if a young person affirms that from now on, he or she will always try hard at school and restrain himself or herself from making offensive remarks, then the leader puts the statement into perspective and suggests that he or she choose a day and lesson when he or she will restrain himself or herself. Everything that the participants in the

Mythodrama enact or express could contain a hint about how to proceed concretely. The concrete changes are derived from the story endings, plays, drawings, and subsequent discussions. The Mythodrama searches for hints in everything the participants produce. The courage students mobilize in their final play to oust a tyrant might serve as a template for internal squabbles and power struggles, or the interpretation of a drawing gives a hint that the concrete change can be carried out with the help of conversation.

To talk about change is one thing; to carry out a change is more difficult. We all have good intentions and might want to better ourselves until reality strikes. Often, our habits are stronger than our good intentions. We are confronted with our limits, laziness, and lack of determination. After all, problems are often already an expression of the limits of our self-control. We resolve to drink less, but if there is a glass of red wine on the table, it would be a sin not to sip it. Resolutions therefore do not lead to a reprogramming of our behaviour. We must also reckon with our addictions, desires, urges, complexes, and feelings. However, resolutions and intentions are still important because they indicate the direction we should follow in our in concrete actions.

Some resolutions are an attempt to save face. When we realise that maybe we do behave according to our conscious values, our self-image is in jeopardy. We might get in trouble with ourselves. We either revise our self-image, or we might have to start to doubts about our self-concept. In order to save our self-image, we might construe an excuse. Our positive and socially conforming self-image consequently needs not to be questioned. The deeper reason is our self-image's purpose is to reconcile ourselves with ourselves. Only a positive self-image keeps us going. We make a resolution, but it might just be a temporary attempt to protect us from self-doubts. Intentions therefore often serve to self-soothe. One feels better when one resolves to do more sports, to assert oneself in the face of the boss, or to get up earlier. What we fantasize about ourselves becomes a personality trait that we attribute to ourselves. Many resolutions are meant for our own ears or serve as absolution, a short-term self-exaltation.

However, resolutions can also initiate real changes. If a resolution is meant seriously, then it might be a first step towards overcoming a problem. There are certain factors one should take into consideration. First of all, the resolution should be emotionally loaded. It should be more than just an idea. When the resolution is energized from within, there is a bigger chance that it will result in a change of behaviour and perception. Our personal psyche or that of a group we belong to is engaged. For example, if a young person resolves to tame his tantrums in class, it helps when the resolution corresponds with an inner scenario. The youngster creates an appealing image of himself or herself. He or she manages his or her tantrums because an imagination provides him or her with the necessary power. The leader must keep this in mind while he or she is evaluating the ideas the participants produce during Mythodrama. He or she must be convinced that the roles children choose in play and scenarios contain valuable clues about how to proceed with a challenge or problem. The concrete changes are then the expression and realization of imagined scenes.

Concrete change means that something in the environment or behaviour changes that uninvolved outside persons register. It should be noticeable, even if one is not informed about the resolution. However, the change does not imply that it solves the respective problem immediately. The change should trigger a process that ultimately leads to an acceptable situation or permanent solution of the problem. It initiates a new approach to the problem in question. In the aforementioned class, eating pizza was a first attempt to reduce tension among students and improve work attitudes.

Concrete changes, however, are not always related to the child or adolescent's external environment. They may also have to do with a subjective issue. The change then refers to a personal issue or challenge. Often, it is about how one deals with oneself, what image one cultivates about oneself, and what mental images one adheres to. For example, a teenage boy who had motivational problems at school and was always fighting with his parents about it developed an idea of who and how he wanted to be thanks to Mythodrama. He saw himself as a scientist in a research laboratory at the ETH (Swiss Federal Institute of Technology). This idea was attractive to him. It led him to try hard in school and not to get lost in partying. Thanks to this distant goal and his new image of himself, school effort was easier for him. He understood his school efforts as preparatory actions for his later career or social role. One girl identified with a character in the story presented. She saw herself as a prima donna. Identifying with this figure gave her the strength to join her peers, socialize, and stand by herself. The figure of the prima donna, paraphrased in a story, became her role model.

The children or teenagers attend the Mythodrama sessions because they are confronted with a problem or challenge. They have to bear trouble and strive at home, they might suffer because of a trauma, are trying to cope with depression, are disorientated in their lives, are prone to violence, tend to bully their schoolmates or behave rebelliously at school. Ergo, they experience their everyday lives and consequently themselves as problematic. This experience determines their perception. They are annoyed by themselves and often angry at their environment. This experience becomes an internal default. They search for reasons for their unsatisfactory condition. They hope to be able to blame their environment, fellow human beings, and sometimes themselves. This leads to a lack of awareness. We get caught up in ourselves. In situations like this, we search for explanation, which rectify us. When, according to their view, their environment is to blame, they fail to detect other friendly qualities. They are unable to detect the friendliness in the gaze of a teacher; instead, they are convinced they are again being controlled viciously. They perceive their environment according to their prevailing pattern. The negative self-attribution is the result of experience, but it can also be triggered by a diagnosis. If they have been labeled as an ADHD'er or are accused of lacking communication skills, they perceive themselves accordingly. They are trapped. Positive feedback or successes are not acknowledged because they remain fixated on the negative or personal deficits. Therefore, the concrete change aims at releasing the child or the group from a negative loop. The intention is to recall and implement the ideas and responses imagined and discussed during the Mythodrama session. Hopefully, the change triggers a change in attitude and perception. For example, a child is then reminded that he or she is an explorer by rearranging the furniture in his room and hanging up a poster of a sailing ship. A superficial change, but it might correspond to an inner transformation. He or she is reminded, that he or she doesn't need to see himself or herself as a problematic ADHD'er, but as a human who is curious about what is going on in this world. In crisis intervention in school, the particular classes should no longer accept the tag that they are "the most difficult class in the schoolhouse," but may perceive themselves as the coolest class of the school!

Patience is important during this work. The specific change is merely the first step toward improvement, a kick-start. The concrete change should initiate a process to gain more self-confidence and mobilize energy so that the child or adolescent finally solves his or her problem. This approach needs obduracy. Also, we must be critical of ourselves and modest. Often, we are convinced that we know the right answer. For example, if a child suffers from school phobia or is being bullied by schoolmates, then, of course, we want the situation to change quickly. The child should be comforted, learn to defend himself or herself, and the culprit must be apprehended. We want the mental health of the victim to improve. We yearn for quick fixes. In campaigns against drugs, for example, the slogan "Just say no!" was a key phrase of an advertising campaign against drugs in the 1980s by the Reagan administration. The notion was that you can make a conscious decision against drugs. However, mental problems and social difficulties rarely disappear thanks to willpower.[1] In most cases, it is necessary to overcome inner and outer resistance and to work through complexes before improvement occurs. As therapists, we must therefore practice modesty and restraint. The danger is that we impose solutions on the child or family that they are not able to execute for psychological reasons. We raise false hopes. It is therefore important to communicate clearly that the implementation of a concrete change does not mean that the problem is solved. Solving psychological problems requires time and dedication but also confidence. Concrete changes are small, modest alterations in the rhythm of life, in attitudes or everyday actions, but they might have an impact on the people involved. A first step has been taken to solve the problem. These circumstances must be communicated to the leader of the Mythodrama, to the parents, and, of course, to the affected child or group. Mythodrama does not produce instant successes, but unblocks the persons or group concerned so that they activate their inner resources and recognise opportunities.

The leaders often experience the transfer phase as stressful. The reason is they must change the mind of the individual or the group. The Mythodrama leader demands that the solutions found in the story be transferred to the realities of their lives. One leaves the lightness of life and is confronted with facts by returning to the initial problem. The participants or the individual are reminded of their problem by the Mythodrama leader. He or she asks them to relate their dramatizations, drawings, and conversations to the reality of their lives. Their imaginations are considered as a source for new ideas and to find new solutions and strategies. For example, when children play at rescuing a colleague from a Mafia dungeon with laser guns, the conclusion points to the importance of teamwork and solidarity. The leader then considers working on the team spirit of class in order to help them to cope with their difficult situation. If a child fantasizes that he or she is standing on a mountain, strapped on a flying machine that then takes him or her for a ride over a swamp, this might be a hint that aloofness is important and he or she needs to trust his or her crazy ideas more. Imaginations and games serve as a fund of ideas for possible changes. These are not always obvious but become apparent after having done interpretations.

By deriving the change from the individual's or group's imagination, the likelihood that it will be successful increases. The resolution is based on a self-developed mental conception. The effort corresponds to an inner willingness. This increases the chance that the change will be executed and the problem solved.

Not every Mythodrama session results in a change, though. In ongoing therapy groups, it makes no sense to aim for a change in every session. To emphasize a change only makes sense when solving a specific problem or issues is paramount. In ongoing groups, the meaning of the images and the acted scenes are discussed without envisaging a concrete change.

ENDNOTES

[1] S. Lilienfeld & H. Arkowitz, *Why 'Just Say No' Doesn't Work.*

Epilogue

In this last chapter I will say a few words about the main characteristics and a peculiarity of Mythodrama.

Psychotherapy is often accused of operating in a space disconnected from reality. The actual behaviour of the clients is not discussed but rather the subjective reports and in many cases distorted narratives of the patients. The allegation is that psychotherapists mistake these accounts with reality. The sufferings, worries, and supposed culprits the patients about talk about are taken as factual. When the particular narratives are not questioned, this might lead to false conclusions. Sometimes these criticisms might be justified, but basically, they derive from a misunderstanding. Psychotherapists' job it not to clarify the truth of their patients' statements and impressions unless they have an expert assignment. The accounts and reports told to them are seen as a mirror of their psyche. The main purpose of psychotherapist is to search for clues to understand the inner world of the patient. So when the psychotherapist hears that mother was depressed, the husband's family is hostile, he or she was bullied for no reason at all, he or she might perceive it as an objective report, but more importantly, it is the way the patient experiences his or her surroundings. As stated, diagnoses are not objective either. They are based primarily on impressions left during an individual therapeutic setting. The quality of the relation to the psychotherapist and the setting influence the assessment. The rule of abstinence and the confidence principle make it impossible for psychotherapists to make a comprehensive assessment of the patient's personal environment. It is not their job to verify the patient's statements. When working with adults, one cannot take a trip down memory lane and ask a patient's mother if she really neglected her daughter or ask the employer why the patient was fired. The goal of psychotherapy is to help patients deal with themselves and their challenges. Psychotherapy is therefore *one-sided* and must not presume to give an objective assessment of the background, causes, social context, and aftereffects of a patient's past. Especially in individual work, one remains in a space sealed off from other realities of life. The therapeutic imperative of confidentiality prohibits us from matching the patient's information with people he or she relates to if he or she does not wish to do so.

The systematic exclusion of other perceptions about the patient and the verification of the statements is the strength of psychotherapy. It enables the person in question to sort out life from within himself or herself, to search for his or her own resources, and to develop a strategy that is in tune with his or her own personality. Psychotherapy offers a space for a temporary time-out, where one's own self comes to the fore, neither social convention, other opinions, morals, nor social expectations play a role. One can free oneself from problematic effects of one's own history or life situation and redesign one's life.

However, the situation is different with children and with conflict work. The reality of life cannot be ignored. When working as a school psychologist, social educator, psychologist, and often also as a psycho-therapist, we are confronted with situations in which the starting point of our work is not the index patient but an overall problem. The therapy is initiated by an outside authority. A young person is sent to us because he or she tends to throw tantrums at home and the parents don't know what to do, internal tensions escalate in a school class, bullying occurs, or a child suffers from the effects of a parent's alcoholism or because of incidents of violence. It is not possible to focus only on the inner world and the descriptions of the child or adolescent; the wishes and concerns of other people must also be considered. We need to think in systems, identify role allocations, and take into account collective dynamics. Usually, we are confronted with various and often contradicting views and personalities. It becomes difficult to do justice to everyone involved. It is no longer just about the inner world and one person's account of the outer world, but we are confronted with different inner worlds and often contradictory accounts of what is happening on the outside. As psychotherapists, we are in danger of becoming one-sided and thus unfair, or of drawing banal conclusions. A quarreling team of teachers is told that they should communicate without being aggressive, or parents are told that the puberty of their own children is a challenge for them. The danger is that the conclusions will not bring any added value for the people concerned because they are too unspecific.

Mythodrama attempts to solve this dilemma using stories. The story transfers the problem or issue into a topos that is foreign to everyone involved. Nobody has prior knowledge and can draw immediate conclusions. Everybody is mentally transferred to another realm and starts anew. They dedicate themselves to the story. However, the choice of story is not random. It is chosen after a careful analysis of the conflict or issue. This trick makes it easier for everyone to get a comprehensive impression and to integrate the diverse positions. Mythodrama is therefore suitable for work with children and adolescents but also for therapies with families, the facilitation of teamwork, or in conflicts.

The Mythodrama sessions described in the book are characterised by three core features: Conflict Acceptance, Imagination, and Social Skills Improvement. Mythodrama allows a process during which the participants enact and work through conflicts without consciously being aware of it. The participants dive into a story and then playfully enact its imagined continuation. Mythodramatic groups, therefore, often seem a bit chaotic, and the outcomes are unpredictable. Mythodrama groups don't follow a predefined program because they should be open for unexpected issues. Because of this semi-chaos procedure, it is more likely that complexes, frustrations, and fears manifest themselves without anybody being aware of it. Mythodramas proceed within an orderly framework, though, and are characterized by a fixed sequence of events; this minimal structuring allows for surprises and the outburst of hidden emotions and fantasies. The participants are not disciplined but are integrated into an event through the structure, the attention to the story, and the sequence of events. This gives them the freedom to express themselves bluntly without creating chaos. They get involved. Of course, as I will show, this often leads to anger, aggression, and unexpected emotions. Often the group leader gets involved in conflicts. A girl is offended and protests because she cannot choose the story herself; a boy begins to brag and talk badly about the leaders; or a girl treats her colleague disparagingly. Conflicts occur during the sessions. These are important because they are manifestations of the complexes and frustrations of the attendants.

The second feature is imagination. Thanks to the use of stories, mental movers, and a playful element, participants develop fantasies. Imagination is understood as a *resource* and a method to manage conflicts and solve problems. As illustrated in the book, our imaginations are often at odds with the expectations and demands of our social environment. We must function, respect codes and taboos, and fulfill role expectations. Being part of a society means conforming with and obliging to the respective rules. In order to comply, we need to dissociate ourselves from parts of our personality. We focus on our duties and tasks and consequently often fail to realise that there is another program running inside us, goals, desires, frustrations, fantasies, dreams we repress. Mythodrama tries to tap into these hidden assets to evolve new ways to cope with challenges and solve problems.

The last achievement of mythodramatic groups is the promotion of *social competence*. This is, of course, especially the case with children and adolescents. A great deal happens in mythodramatic groups among the participants themselves. The leaders might even not be aware of the array of different interactions. The children or adolescents get angry, excited, worried, aggressive; they are ashamed, delighted, amazed, or confused. During the group sessions, we are confronted with diverse patterns of behaviour. As they abandon the adaptation mode they usually show at school, spontaneous behaviors emerge. They take the mask off, they tend to put on when adults are present, and they present themselves the way they behave among colleagues, at school, and often at home. The decisive factor is that the group leaders are present, but they do not dominate the interactions. The group leaders therefore often become witnesses to inappropriate, crude, and often indecent behaviour on the part of the children or young people. In groups, there is a lot of swearing, cursing, provoking, and remarks made that even make adults blush. Even young children might use coarse, sexually explicit language. Since they believe they are among themselves, they lose their restraint. They feel protected by the group situation. It is not the adults who dominate. As a rule, the children or adolescents have built up a relationship with the group leaders, though. Even when they do not define what happens, they remain important reference persons. They observe and interfere when they children have gone too far. They intervene when a child pushes a colleague violently, insults him or her, or obstructs the storytelling. The children are being made aware of etiquette and manners. Often, however, the groups establish rules of conduct themselves. In school crisis interventions, conclusions are even deliberately expected of the students. They must decide on a change that they implement in their class. Mythodramatic groups therefore promote social skills. The children or young people learn how to behave even when the watchful eye of adults is not on them. Not only do the group leaders become role models, but also the experiences the children and adolescents make help them to develop social skills.

References

Aichinger, A. & Holl, W. (2010). *Gruppentherapie mit Kindern. Kinderpsychodrama*, Band 1. Wiesbaden: VS Verlag.

Aichinger, A. (2010). *Gruppentherapie mit Kindern*. Wiesbaden: Verlag für Sozialwissenschaften.

Anzieu, D. (1996, 2016). *Le groupe et l'inconscient*. Paris: Payot. English: *The Group and the Unconscious*. Milton-Park: Taylor and Francis.

Campbell, J. (1949). *The Hero with a Thousand Faces*. Princeton, New Jersey: Bollingen Series, Princeton University Press.

Darwin, C. (2003). *The Origin of Species*. London: Penguin.

Fichte, J.G. (1974). *Grundlage der gesamten Wissenschaftslehre als Handschrift für seine Zuhörer (1794)*. Hamburg: Meiner.

Frances, A. (2013). *Saving Normal*. New York: HarperCollins.

Gelernter, D. (2016). *The Tides of Mind. Uncovering the Spectrum of Consciousness*. New York: Liveright Publishing.

Goffmann, E. (1959). *The Presentation of the Self in Everyday Life*. New York: Doubleday.

Gottschall, J. (2012). *The Storytelling Animal. How Stories Make Us Human*. New York: Mariner Books.

Guggenbühl, A. (1993). *Die unheimliche Faszination der Gewalt*. Zürich: Edition IKM (vormals Raben-Reihe: www.ikm.ch).

Guggenbühl, A. (1998). *Das Mythodrama. Eine Untersuchung über ein gruppentherapeutisches Verfahren bei Kindern aus Scheidungsfamilien*. Zürich: Edition IKM.

Guggenbühl, A. (2001). *Wer aus der Reihe tanzt, lebt intensiver. Mut zum persönlichen Skandal*. München: Kösel.

Guggenbühl, A. (2002). Dem Dämon in die Augen schauen: Kriseninterventionen in der Schule. In M. Drilling & H. Wehrli (Hrsg.), *Gewalt in Schulen: Ursachen, Prävention, Intervention* (S. 130–135). Zürich: Verlag Pestalozzianum.

Haidt, J. (2006). *The Happiness Hypothesis*. New York: Basic Books.

Hell, D. (2013). *Krankheit als seelische Herausforderung*. Basel: Schwabe.

Huxley, T.H. (1863). *Evidence as to Man's Place in Nature*. London: Williams and Norgate.

Kast, V. (1988). *Imagination als Raum der Freiheit*. Olten: Walter-Verlag.

Konner, M. (2010). *The Evolution of Childhood*. Cambridge: Harvard University Press.

Leuner, H. & Wilke, E. (2005). *Katathym-imaginative Psychotherapie*. Stuttgart: Thieme.

Lilienfeld, S.O. & Arkowitz, H. (2014). *Why 'Just Say No' Doesn't Work*. Scientific American.

Lim, M. & Mynier, K. (1993). "Effect of server posture on restaurant tipping," *Journal of Applied Social Psychology*, Vol. 23, Issue 8 April 1993.

Miller, A. (2008). *The Drama of the Gifted Child.* New York: Basic Books.

Morgan, J.J.B. (1931). *Child Psychology*, New York: Richard R Smith Incorp.

Murray, D. (2019). *The Madness of Crowds. Gender, Race and Identity*. London: Bloomsberry Continuum.

Oatley, K. (2001). *Such Stuff as Dreams. The Psychology of Fiction.* New York: Wiley.

Paris, G. (2007). *Wisdom of Psyche*. London: Routledge.

Pinker, S. (1997). *How the Mind Works*. New York: Norton.

Radin, P. (1970). *The Winnebago Tribe*. Lincoln, Nebraska: Bison Books.

Reddemann, L. & Stasing, J. (2013). *Imagination*. Tübingen: Psychotherapie-Verlag.

Reddemann, L. (2013). *Imagination als heilsame Kraft*. Stuttgart: Klett-Cotta.

Rose, T. (2015). *The End of Average. How to Succeed in a World that Values Sameness*. New York: HarperCollins.

Salinger, J. D. (1951). *The Catcher in the Rye*. London: Penguin.

Schiefele, U., Schreyer, I. (1994). Intrinsische Lernmotivation und Lernen, *Zeitschrift für Pädagogische Psychologie*.

References

Schreiber, F.R. (1973). *The Many Faces of Sybil.* Washington, DC: Henry Regnery Company.

Schulte-Sasse, J. (2001). Einbildungskraft/Imagination. In: K. Barck, M. Fontius, D. Schlenstedt, B. Steinwachs & F. Wolfzettel (Eds.), *Ästhetische Grundbegriffe.* (S.88 - 120) Stuttgart: J.B. Metzler.

Shackleton, E. H. (1910). *The Heart of Antarctic.* Heinemann: London.

Singer, J. L. & Pope, K. S. (1978). *The Power of Human Imagination.* New York: Plenum Press.

Slavson, S. R. & Schiffer, M. (1976). *Gruppenpsychotherapie mit Kindern.* Göttingen: Vandenhoeck und Ruprecht.

Sodendorf, T. (2013). *The Gap: The Science of What Separates Us from Other Animals.* New York: Basic Books.

Solms, M. (2022). *The Hidden Spring. A Journey to the Source of Consciousness,* New York: Norton.

Stevens, A. (2006). "The Archetypes," Ed. Papadopoulos, Renos, *The Handbook of Jungian Psychology.* London: Routledge.

Suddendorf, T. (2013). *The Gap: the Science of What Separates Us From Other Animals.* New York: Basic Books.

Suddendorf, T. (2014). *Der Unterschied – Was den Menschen zum Menschen macht.* Berlin: Berlin-Verlag.

Sunstein, C.R. (2003). *Why Societies Need Dissent.* Cambridge: Harvard University Press.

von Schaik, C. & Michel, K. (2016). *The Good Book about Human Nature.* Brentwood, TN: Hachette Group Book.

von Scotti, A. (2016). *Nur Sommer: Irische-schottische Kirche.* Borsdorf: Winterwork.

Wallace, A.R. (1855). "On the law which has regulated the introduction of new species,." *Annals and Magazine of Natural History*, Vol. 16 (2nd Series), September.

Waters, E. (2010). *Crazy Like Us. The Globalization of the American Psyche.* New York: Free Press.

Wilson, D. S. (2003). *Darwin's Cathedral.* Chicago: University of Chicago Press.

Zahavi, D. (2014). *Self and Other. Exploring Subjectivity, Empathy and Shame.* Oxford: Oxford University Press.

www.ingramcontent.com/pod-product-compliance
Lightning Source LLC
Chambersburg PA
CBHW020705270326
41928CB00005B/271